Assembling Again

Peter Mullen

Edward Arnold

© Peter Mullen 1979

First published 1979
by Edward Arnold (Publishers) Ltd
41 Bedford Square, London WC1B 3DQ

British Library Cataloguing in Publication Data

Mullen, Peter
　Assembling again.
　1. Worship programs
　I. Title
　377'.1　　　　　BV283.S3

ISBN 0-7131-0387-6

Set in Garamond 11 on 12 point by Unwin Brothers Limited,
The Gresham Press, Old Woking, Surrey and
Printed in Great Britain by
Spottiswoode Ballantyne Limited,
Colchester and London.

Contents

iv

Introduction

I had no idea when I set down my first series of short talks in *'Assembling'* that within a year I should be asked for more. This does not mean that the first set of talks were necessarily the answer to *every* headteacher's prayer. But the popularity of *'Assembling'* shows I was right about one thing: the *need* for assembly material.

So now we are *'Assembling Again'* and I would add to what I said in the introduction to the first book only an emphasis on the *flexibility* of these pieces. They can be used in at least four or five different ways.

First, each talk can simply be read as it stands. They are designed for immediate communication.

Or a teacher might wish to skim through the book until some suitable topic presents itself and then, using the ideas and information provided, give a short talk in his own words.

Or again, the pieces might suggest possible ways of pupil participation in the form of dialogue, interviews or even short dramatic representations of individual themes.

The talks are meant to appeal to pupils of secondary school age and to deal with subjects of teenage interest. They are also meant to give a certain amount of information and to stimulate discussions and questions. In this way *'Assembling Again'* might be used to some profit in everyday class teaching of RE.

While 'films, pop and television' are prominently featured so that the attention of the young audience may be grasped from the start, I have this time included sections on the more familiar events in the life of Jesus. For example, the teacher will have no difficulty in finding four or five talks which taken together make up a programme for the week before Easter holidays. The same is true for Christmas.

For this purpose and for many others, my publishers wisely suggested the provision of not *one* index but *three*.

As with *'Assembling'* the talks are not dogmatic nor do they follow any party line. You will not find here an attempt to 'ram religion down their throats.' But these pieces are designed to provoke discussion and, of course, the first prerequisite of discussion is disagreement. He who said 'The *fact* of disagreement is the *beginning* of education' was, perhaps, not very wide of the mark. I hope you will find much here with which you are in agreement—and perhaps even more with which you can profitably beg to differ!

PETER MULLEN

Absurdity and the Spanner

Some days are perfect. You awake at eight o'clock. Breakfast tastes good. It's sunny. There's no school because it's the middle of August. By five past nine you've got a bag full of sandwiches. One pound and eighty-five pence and you're off to the test match. It doesn't rain. England bat. At lunch they're ninety-nine for none and at close of play three hundred and twelve for three—an almost unbeatable position. Home by seven-thirty, a meal then sit by the television. And what d'you think? Here's a close up in edited highlights of all the exciting events in the day's play.

What a pity not all days are like this. How about January twenty-eighth. Pouring with rain. Get up late. Miss breakfast. Fall running for school bus. Mud all over English homework—only half finished anyway. Games cancelled because the pitch is waterlogged. Old so-and-so the English teacher makes you do the work again. Then when you finally return home your mother has left you a cold tea and instructions to light the fire.

Mind you it's a good job days aren't usually as extreme as these. As a rule there's a bit of good and a bit of bad in every twenty-four hours. Sometimes things go according to plan. Occasionally everything gets snarled up.

Some thinkers called nihilists say 'Everything's meaningless'. They reckon that nothing counts for anything in the end. That life is just a series of pleasant or unpleasant happenings. They even say that 'pleasant' and 'unpleasant' don't stand for anything that really matters. Nothing matters. 'It's all absurd' they say.

Well you know how it's sometimes said of a thing ruined, 'someone threw a spanner in the works'? You know, wrecked it? Let's have a go at throwing a spanner in the absurdists' direction: If *everything's* absurd, then the absurdists' statement that 'everything is absurd' is also absurd. And of course we won't believe him because you *wouldn't* believe something that was absurd would you? And if the opposite is true—'everything's not absurd' then we can go on looking for meaning and purpose in life—even in school life on a wet day in January.

Please God, restore our confidence when we think that everything is pointless and absurd. Give us courage when things go against us. Amen.

1

An Altogether Different Omnibus

There's a time of day and a season of the year that are absolutely impossible. That's when you leave the house at five past eight in the morning, second week in January to go and queue for the school bus. It's still dark. It's raining or slushy and one shoe lets in a bit of the wet. And then the bus is late because of the weather. Or it comes and it's full and you have to wait for the next one. That means you'll be late for school and the form teacher or a prefect will tell you off. And you can't convince them it wasn't your fault you were late. How awful waiting for a bus can be.

And yet it might all be very different. In the middle of Leeds at a place called the Corn Exchange you can catch a late night bus to the suburbs. Waiting for that bus is marvellous even if you're all by yourself. That's because there's no rush and also because while you're waiting you can watch the flickering repetitive lights of the large outdoor advertisements. There used to be one of a seal knocking a ball under a glass of beer to another seal at the other side. It was only a series of electric light bulbs really but it looked good—warm, friendly, alive. You could have a private bet with yourself how many times the ball would pass between the seals before the bus came.

And you'd feel good anyway because you'd just been to a film or a show. Perhaps to a dance. Now the odd thing is the registration number of the late night bus might show that it's one you often catch for school in the morning. But at that time of night . . . an altogether different omnibus.

Heavenly Father, thank you for enjoyable journeys and for those who rise early and take late rest so that we may travel home. Amen.

Arnold and the Tone Row

Musicians among you will know all about key signatures. Even if you're not a practising pianist, violinist or singer it's likely that you've heard announcers on the radio introducing pieces of music. And they often say something ending with ' . . . number 5 by Beethoven in C Minor' or '23 in A by Mozart.' The letters 'C' and 'A' stand for the keys in which the music is written. There are forty-eight keys altogether in music. That includes the bright keys called 'major' and the more melancholy ones known as 'minor'.

It's hard to say exactly what's meant by a key except that it's based on a note to which any particular tune belongs. Perhaps the best way to understand what a key means is through hearing someone play or sing 'off-key' or 'out of key'. This is a really shocking experience because when we start listening to a tune we expect it to go in a recognisable direction and when it doesn't we feel like protesting, 'Ouch! That was a wrong note.'—almost as if we've experienced a physical pain. But we only think this way because in pop and classical music it's what we're used to. There's nothing sacred or unalterable about key signatures. You can write music that takes no notice of keys at all if you wish.

In 1908 a composer called Arnold Schoenberg wrote some music which ignored keys. And, as you might expect, to those who'd been trained to listen to tunes in the old fashioned way—and that meant almost everybody—it sounded shocking, tuneless, like a rattling of tin cans. But Schoenberg persisted and developed a new style of music called 'Twelve Tone', and today most of the pieces being written are more or less based on his system.

Which ought to caution us against writing off anything new until we've really tried to understand what the innovator is up to. That goes for new work in the arts and the sciences alike.

Almighty God, thank you for those who find new ways of expressing old truths. Amen.

Beating Boredom

It's impossible to imagine a Manchester United football fan being bored as he watches his team score the winning goal in a cup-tie. Fanatical? Beside himself? Shouting? Cheering? Jumping up and down? All these things perhaps. But certainly not boredom.

You can understand someone getting bored stiff in the middle of a difficult maths exercise last thing on a Thursday afternoon. Even geography can be just a little bit boring—if you're studying the coastline of South America and you can hear your friends playing tennis or cricket in the sweltering sun. Anybody who's ever had to swot for a July exam knows how tedious revision can be on a hot day.

But you wouldn't be bored crossing the tape to win a race for your school, county or country. The very daydream of doing this is exciting never mind the real thing. Many folks wouldn't hear a brass band at full volume while they were reading their favourite book. And you couldn't be bored eating your first choice food in an expensive restaurant.

It's worth asking what makes some things boring and others just the opposite. Someone who wasn't interested in football wouldn't necessarily share the Manchester United supporter's joy at seeing the winning goal. He might say 'I don't like football. I couldn't care less if they win or lose. Who's playing anyway?' And no doubt there are some foods you might find absolutely uninteresting—like fish fingers perhaps—but which your younger brother would devour in a frenzy.

It goes to show that it's not *things* that are boring. Goals and tennis and fish fingers might fascinate you but make someone else switch off completely. We find life interesting and worthwhile if we actually involve ourselves in it. Really *do* something. Make an effort. You'll notice that the liveliest people are those who are interested in the most things.

Heavenly Father, help us to get involved in the day's events so that we may enjoy life to the full. Amen.

Becoming Mr. Klee

When you're young, parents and teachers are always trying to discover what you want to do later in life. So they ask, 'What are you going to be when you leave school?' And 'What do you want to be?' They mean, of course, 'What do you want to do for a living?' There's more to individuals than the jobs they do between nine and five.

One cheeky answer to the question 'What do you want to be?' is 'A person, what d'you think?' And this answer doesn't entirely miss the point either because in a way you're not going to *be* anything other than a person when you're older. Bigger and stronger. More experienced perhaps. But this doesn't mean you're going to alter your basic being as a person.

In another sense, though, the word 'being' is less important than another word 'becoming'. The artist Paul Klee wrote in his diary in 1914 'What is really essential, really productive is the way—after all, Becoming is Superior to Being.' That ancient old Greek Plato said something similar many hundreds of years before Paul Klee was born. He said 'To be perfect is to have changed often.' Both sayings should encourage us not to become set in our ways, determined we'll never change because that's the way to boredom. That's the way we become old before we're young—dead even before we've ever really lived.

But the Way of becoming, of leaving yourself open to the future and prepared to change your mind and your opinions from time to time needs great courage. Christians can draw some help in this from the New Testament where St. John reports Jesus as saying 'I am the Way . . .'

This doesn't mean we have an easy passage through life, that Jesus will do everything for us and make things less difficult. It does mean that one way of becoming, of leaving oneself open to the future, is to follow the example of Jesus who was always prepared to be led by the spirit.

Heavenly Father, teach us to face the future with courage and faith. Amen.

Bent Spoons and the Stars

Have you ever bent a spoon? Not by tapping it on an egg laid by a hen who had eaten too much iron, but by magic? It's a serious question because you've no doubt heard of one person who used to bend spoons all the time—Uri Geller. And he could bend them without even needing to touch them. Not only that, but he could stop watches ticking—even watches that weren't in the same room as himself. More sensational still, Mr. Geller did his tricks over the television so that if you happened to be watching his programme the clocks in your house might come to a stop. And spoons bend in the kitchen drawer.

No one knows how he did it. Some think he used special powers but others say it was all just a trick. What interested everybody at the time was the idea that if Uri Geller was using special powers then the universe must be a far more mysterious place than ordinary science teaches us.

Those who believed that Uri Geller wasn't just a trickster tried to convince us that the amazing things he could do with spoons and watches were signs to us all that there were secret powers at work in the universe—even that they proved the existence of God.

We always seem to want miraculous signs of this kind before we'll believe anything. Ralph Waldo Emerson knew this but he wrote:

'If the stars should appear one night in a thousand years, how would men believe and adore!'

And by this he meant to say that we're blind to the signs of wonder—even of God's existence—that are around us all the time. Like the stars. We always look for novelties and strange occurrences. Perhaps if we look at the world around us more thoughtfully we'll see wonders enough. Just as an afterthought : Isn't it a good thing that most spoons *don't* bend unless you squeeze them?

Heavenly Father, thank you for the signs and wonders that are around us all the time. For the night sky. For seas and sunsets. Also for the ordinariness and friendliness of things. Amen.

Bet on Eternity

One of the basic questions in life is whether when we die that's all there is to it. Do we just snuff out? Is this life all we have? Or is there something else? As on many other issues, opinions are divided. Some say that we remember nothing from the time before we were born simply because we didn't exist before that. And that the same goes for the time after we die. Our life is here. It lasts perhaps seventy years and then it's over.

But other people believe in heaven or hell and they say that everyone will eventually go to one of these places depending on whether he's done good or bad in this life.

Whichever view you take, it's a personal matter. No one can force you to believe one thing or the other. Some folks believe that we come back in another form—perhaps as dogs or bees. So there's plenty of scope for thought.

Blaise Pascal was a man who couldn't bring himself to think that this life is all we have. He claimed that a God of Love wouldn't permit us to be extinguished like so many dead matches. Pascal was even prepared to bet on the after-life. Crazy? So you might think. But after a bit more consideration Pascal's bet may not be as silly as it sounds.

For he argued, 'If I bet on an after-life and I'm right, then that's marvellous and I win the bet. If, on the other hand, I'm wrong, then I'll never know anything about it—not even that I was wrong.'

No doubt there's more to religious faith than placing bets but Pascal's wager has a logic about it which many people have found hard to resist.

Heavenly Father, thank you for all the blessings of this life. Give us faith so that we may know that whatever happens, nothing can separate us from your love. Amen.

The Bionic Man

Television once ran a series of episodes about a man who'd lost his arms and legs in a plane crash. He was a test pilot for supersonic aircraft. Instead of supplying him with ordinary artificial limbs, which are never quite as good as the originals, his superiors in the aeroplane industry gave him wonderfully powerful 'bionic' arms and legs. So this test pilot became a kind of superman who, with his new limbs—miracles of science and technology—was the strongest and fastest man in the world.

Of course you couldn't let a man loose if he had this much power. So he was hired to work specially for the government to sniff out and deal with crime and treachery wherever it arose. He could run faster than anyone else too. So that when the bionic man was seen on the move the cameras slowed down his moving image to give an artificial example of pace and power—like they do in action replays of 'Match of the Day'.

The bionic man did a great deal of good, crushing enemies of the state and keeping the peace. Nobody could doubt his value to the country and even to the world. But there's something about him that's not quite right. Not anything that he does, miracles of peace keeping and national defence. But his name. You see when the authorities reconstructed the bionic man after his plane crash it cost them six million dollars. And so he became known as 'The Six Million Dollar Man.' And that's what's wrong. It's false to describe a person by the amount of money he's associated with. We can't make bionic men, but we often refer to people by the money they earn. So you hear people say, 'He's a £10,000 a year man' or 'She gets £100.00 per week' you know.

And this is wrong. Every human being is entitled to the same amount of dignity and respect, for all are equal in the sight of God. Any price we put on a person's character or services is an entirely secondary affair and nothing at all to do with people's value as people.

Almighty God, teach us to value one another as human beings and not to think that we can give everyone a price. Amen.

A bird to Asclepius

What to take for someone who's ill in hospital? Grapes are the favourite—but they're usually eaten by the visitors rather than by the patient. Bottles of orange glucose wrapped in cellophane. Books: not too 'heavy'; not too long. Magazines to while away the time. Crossword puzzles. Then there's the chinese ring game puzzle where you have to try and separate twisted metal shapes—without forcing them.

The ancient Greeks had another idea. Not a gift taken to patients this time but a present from the patient to a god Asclepius once he'd recovered. Maybe this was more than a simple superstition, a thanksgiving for recovery from illness. One Greek teacher—perhaps the most famous of them all—Socrates, said to his friend Crito just before his death: 'Crito, I owe a bird to Asclepius; see that the debt is paid.'

So people have said that by this statement Socrates meant to indicate that all his life had been an illness. Not that he had actually been sick all the time but that there was something about life in general which is like an illness. One we're released from at death.

Now the Christian faith teaches us about heaven—about life with God which can begin in the here and now and continue after death. And it's true there are some preachers who pay so much attention to the life of the world to come that they regard our time here as hardly valuable at all. As if at best it's a trial and at worst an illness—which reminds us of Socrates again.

But the truth is that Christianity says this life, this here and now, is every bit as important as any life of the world to come. The Kingdom of God isn't just pie in the sky when you die. The New Testament

8

teaches us that this world and what we do in it is so important that God himself became man in it. In the person of Jesus. At Christmas. So that whatever happens to us the final truth about life is that it's worthwhile. Not a sickness. Not a waste of time. But a large part of God's purpose for us. And to be enjoyed not simply endured.

Heavenly Father, teach us to live our lives in the knowledge that you made us and wish us to have fellowship with you. Amen.

The Boring Robot

Over the past few years there must have been literally scores of new television programmes. Not just the 'once off' show like the circus or the Bolshoi Ballet but whole new series. Cops and Robbers. Pop singers. Tales of town and country. Historical series about Henry VIII and even long running documentary programmes about religion like 'The Long Search.'

Television companies work in competition of course. And so they're constantly looking for new material yet more exciting, more colourful and usually more expensive. Only by doing that do they think they'll keep the best share of the television audience—that's you and me. T.V. producers know we like novelty. Something 'for a change' as they say.

This is true not just about the telly but in lots of other things too. Take pop music for instance. Many people say, 'Ah but it doesn't last.' Well? So what? Pop music isn't supposed to last. A song comes in at number eighteen one week. Soon it's up to number two or three then within a month or so it's disappeared from the hit parade altogether. We've become tired of it and want something new.

Have you ever wondered why we so quickly tire of what's put in front of us for our entertainment? A writer called Colin Wilson says it's as if we have a robot inside us. As you know, robots are based on computers so they learn very quickly. The one inside us does too. After a couple of hearings the robot has got used to the pop tune. Or after, say, half a dozen showings, it's had enough of the new television series. Then we get bored.

This is only a picture of course. Colin Wilson is saying that it's *as if* we've got a boring robot inside us. And he bases this picture language on the fact that we very soon tire of even the newest things. Christmas toys and games. Books. Playground games. They all go out of fashion so quickly and we are easily bored. Why?

> Heavenly Father, thank you for all things new. Help us to get to know and understand your gifts to us of music and pictures so that we may always bring our newness to them. Amen.

Borrowed Time

Teachers have to get used to pupils coming up and asking if they can lend a pen or a ruler or a protractor. What the pupils mean, of course, and what teachers never seem to tire of reminding them is, 'Can, or even may, I *borrow*' instead of lend. Well you might think it's a small point. After all, if someone's going to lend you something, what's wrong with using the expression 'Can I lend it' It's grammar though. And grammar is established usage turned into a rule. Usually worked out for good reasons but sometimes difficult to follow.

There is another meaning of 'lend' or to be more precise 'Lent'. It's a season of the church's year which runs for six weeks before Easter. It's a time when Christians go in for soul-searching, for self-examination. Some go without luxuries as well and give the money they save to a charitable organisation like 'Christian Aid' or 'The Save the Children Fund.' There's a tradition that Christians don't eat meat during Lent and especially not on Fridays during this six week period. The idea of this penitential time, as it's often called, is that we should look inwards at ourselves and pay attention to our faults trying to remedy them where we can. And also to count our gifts and talents and see how we can best serve God in the world.

If you're not a churchgoer perhaps you don't keep Lent very seriously. But whether you're a regular at the Parish Communion or Morning Service or not you can still benefit from this season of the church's year. Lent gives us a few weeks in which we can go in for a good deal of self examination. Not the selfish activity it might sound. For the more we know about ourselves the better we're able to adjust and apply ourselves to a full and active life. It might be ungrammatical then but perhaps not without meaning to say that Lent is borrowed time.

> Almighty Father, help us to know when to be quiet so that we can hear your voice speaking to us about ourselves and your purpose for us. Amen.

Bultmann and the Light Bulb

In the days of King Arthur, even in the days of your great-grandmother almost everyone believed in God. Many stayed away from church just as they do now, but it would be fair to say that religion was seen to be much more a necessary part of human life than it is today. Everyone was baptised. And the churches were full for the great festivals like Christmas and Easter.

But things have changed. A number of people still believe in God and some still go to church. You can't get away from the fact, though, that there's a different atmosphere or climate of opinion these days. There's a vague but general idea that science has taken over from God. True enough, after Charles Darwin and his *Origin of Species* we no longer believe that the bible story about the creation of the world is true just as it stands, word for word. Some thinkers have gone much further. A professor of religion called Rudolf Bultmann wrote about the miracle stories of the New Testament and here's what he said of them: 'You can't believe that sort of thing in an age of the electric light and the wireless.' 'Wireless'? We call it 'radio' nowadays don't we? Bultmann's point is like one being made by lots of other people in the last quarter of the twentieth century. Roughly it says 'Fair enough, it used to be all right to believe in God but now we've grown up we don't need that sort of superstitious belief any more. Not now we've got science.'

The trouble with that point of view is that it really takes no notice of what scientists have actually revealed to us recently about the universe. Radio telescopes tell us about 'quasars' and 'black holes'. Einstein has written about light being bent by gravity and about 'curved space.' There's even serious *scientific* talk about time flowing backwards and 'anti-matter.' Can we believe *these things* even in an age of electric light and radio? Whatever the truth is, it seems a very dangerous game to come out with hard and fast statements to the effect that God is no more. One thing is certain: the universe is more mysterious, more wonderful than was ever previously imagined. And that's what science has told us in the last hundred years.

Almighty Father, thank you for the wonders of the universe. Amen.

But, First

Young people dallying over their classwork are always being told to 'get on with it!' Sometimes that's not as easy as it sounds. Suppose you're about to paint a picture and you find you haven't exactly the colour you need. Well, you have to go and mix it. You can't start without sickly, luminous green when you're painting a dragon. First you must get the colours you need to convey just the right blend of ugliness and horror.

But at other times the command 'get on with it!' is more than justified. Because there are just a few people who seem to take ages to settle down to their work. Broken, lost or forgotten pencils. No ruler, sir. 'Can you use a compass?' 'Yes if I want to find my way home in the dark. It's *compasses* and you're the one who's supposed to be using them!'

Now you'd think the B.B.C. could get things ready on time—with all their experience and expensive equipment. But just tune in to the early evening news and the magazine programme that follows it at about six o'clock. Here's what you get: 'In tonight's programme we show you how to go seal hunting in Wimbledon, *but first* David's been finding out just exactly what our members of parliament have for lunch. All that's *after* a searching enquiry into obesity and sleeplessness among dormice. *And*, which sock does your husband put on first in the morning. *But first* here's your own regional programme etc.... etc...'

It sometimes takes about three minutes of this kind of thing before the programme actually gets started. The reason they do it, of course, is because they know we're not all interested in everything so they mention as many items as possible so that *one* might attract us and we won't switch off, or switch over to the other side.

This isn't very important when it's just to do with T.V. pro-grammes—though it's annoying and very boring. But it is serious if we catch ourselves living like that all the time—looking forward to one thing in the future. Because the only time we know we've got is in the present. Here and now. It's *now* we must live in. Let's learn to enjoy it then.

Heavenly Father, help us not to be always looking to the next thing but to use the present constructively. Amen.

Children and Dogs

It's a general rule that children enjoy looking after pets and that grown ups like looking after children. Like almost every rule though, there are exceptions to it. There's the R.S.P.C.A. who care for unwanted animals and the N.S.P.C.C. which comes to the aid of children when they're treated badly.

But in most cases bonds of friendship are created between a young person and, say, his pet dog. And immense feelings of comradeship can exist between father and son when they're out fishing together or spending a day at the test match. Mothers and daughters often share the same sort of thing (well at least sometimes!) when they're advising each other about perfume and clothes. All these feelings are part of the warmth which human beings can share, and which can even include animal pets.

So what can we make of a statement like: 'Anyone who hates children and dogs can't be all bad'? What a horrid thing to say! It must have been the cruel remark of some wicked emperor or other. But not so. It was said as a joke by the comedian W. C. Fields. And when he said it, it did make people laugh. Not because human beings are monsters deep down and W. C. Fields spoke the truth—letting the cat out of the bag as you might say. In fact the comedian didn't speak *the* truth at all. He spoke *a* truth. And one of the best ways of making sure that people listen to truths is to make them part of a story or a joke.

Everyone knows that children are not always highly delighted with their pets—especially if the pet is a hamster and it's cage cleaning time. And we know that even the most patient adult sometimes becomes exasperated with children—particularly when he wants 'a bit of peace and quiet'. When we laugh at W. C. Field's joke we're laughing at ourselves. Sometimes that can be a help. We're not always the angels we might make ourselves out to be!

Heavenly Father, help us to see ourselves through your eyes that we may correct our faults with good humour. Amen.

Christmas Humphreys Uses Brass Door Knobs

You can test the truth of that yourselves. It's in a book by Lawrence Le Shan. But you might ask 'What does Christmas Humphreys use brass door knobs for?' and 'How could that be of possible interest to me?' Perhaps it's a piece of snobbery. You know the kind of thing—'Christmas Humphreys uses *brass* door knobs but we, poor creatures, can only afford *wooden* ones.' Or it may be that the mysterious Christmas Humphreys is in reality none other than the masked villain and that he uses the brass door knobs to clonk his victims over the head before making off with the swag.

As a matter of fact Christmas Humphreys uses the door knobs to aid meditation. Mr. Le Shan's book is called *How to Meditate*. Well you might think, 'How odd! How unlikely!' After all meditation is supposed to be a very lofty spiritual activity isn't it and you can't get much more down to earth than brass door knobs. Why doesn't he use a crucifix or some rosary beads—even a statue of Buddha or something holy like that?

Mr. Le Shan explains. He tells us that the aim and secret of meditation is to discipline yourself to think about one thing at once. You know most of the time, if you're ever required to sit quietly, all kinds of dizzy and confusing thoughts come whirling into the head. Well meditation is a special technique, very ancient in origin, to help us clear our minds of clutter and concentrate on one thing only. The effects are very beneficial if you meditate regularly—say for a quarter of an hour each day.

And the reason for choosing a simple object—the brass doorknob is quite straightforward too. Statues, rosaries and crucifixes have all sorts of associations in our minds that they could actually set us thinking in a confused or complicated way when what's wanted is singlemindedness. D'you see how even the most ordinary things are so very often the key to something extraordinary and of great spiritual value.

Heavenly Father, help us to look at ordinary everyday objects and to remember that all things are in your care. Amen.

Classical Laughter

One thing about pop concerts is that they show that music is to be enjoyed. There's always lots of cheering and whistling when the singers take the stage. Stroboscopic light fills the hall with movement and colour. Even the screaming's done out of enjoyment. From looking at pop concerts and festivals you'd be certain to recognise that young people know how to enjoy music.

How different it is at classical concerts! The orchestra and conductor dress up formally and seem to take all the proceedings very seriously indeed. Members of the audience sit ever so sedately and talk in hushed whispers—allowing only disciplined hand clapping as a sign of their approval at the end.

The musical occasions are different of course. And it wouldn't do to have a lot of shouting and dancing during a quiet piece or a gentle lullaby for strings. But to look at the faces of some concert goers who are supposed to be there because they're enjoying the music and you'd think they were being sentenced to excruciating punishment. Surely there's no need to let formality rule out the possibility of a smile of pleasure!

Not everybody behaves as dismally as this though. And in his book *Steppenwolf* Hermann Hesse stresses that such gloom really has no part in music. For towards the end of *Steppenwolf* the greatest composer of all time, Mozart, appears—or perhaps it's his ghost. And Hesse describes and presents him as laughing an irresistible and infectious laughter. That seems to fit more appropriately with inspiring music—not gloom but joy. Hesse's vision of Mozart is correct. Certainly the composer of delights like *The Magic Flute* would not have us sulk at his concerts.

Heavenly Father, thank you for all kinds of music. Amen.

Creative Evolution

Anyone who knows anything about biology and natural history has heard of Charles Darwin. He lived in the nineteenth century and made it his business to try and find out how animals and humans developed into the creatures they are today. Briefly his conclusion was that men and women aren't really different in kind from animals. We're just different in degree. That's to say we're more intelligent, more advanced but if you trace the story back into history you'll find that we developed or evolved from animals.

There's nothing very striking or new about this in our day. Almost everyone is familiar with what's come to be known as evolution. But when Darwin wrote his book *The Origin of Species* in 1859 and another book *The Descent of Man* in 1872 some people were upset and outraged by what they read.

Many wouldn't believe Darwin at all. They said that men and women weren't descended from monkeys but were created in the garden of Eden as Adam and Eve. Churchpeople in particular, including bishops, were annoyed at what Darwin had written.

Nowadays we know differently of course. And you won't find many people who believe that there really was a man called Adam and his wife called Eve. We accept that this Bible story is a colourful legend, a myth or a parable which wasn't even meant to be true in the literal historical sense even when it was first written.

And thanks to many modern writers, among them a Frenchman called Henri Bergson, we know that evolution need not be a dull mechanical process at all but a vital, living, creative progression involving God himself. And that creative evolution is a day by day development of the personality of God in our widening understanding.

Almighty God, please use us in all that we do, in all we are and are becoming, in order to reveal your will. Amen.

Dante's Middle State

Lots of writers and painters have given us their picture of what's in store for us in the next life. The writer Dante offered three books. One called *Inferno* tells all about hell. *Paradise* is about heaven. And the third, called *Purgatory* describes a state in between these two. No one really knows whether what Dante wrote has any existence in fact. But his books are very interesting for the kinds of worlds they picture.

Perhaps it's wrong to say so, but Dante's heaven—that's *Paradise*—isn't all that interesting as places go. In one picture of it there are hundreds of stars in tidy crescent arrangement around the sun. They all look alike. The sun is meant to represent God and the stars are the souls of individual men and women in heaven. But that's just what's wrong.

They're all exactly similar. No individuality left. No marking off you as 'you' and me as 'me'. Surely God doesn't want us all to be just the same as each other in every way—like tiny stars from a distance.

Hell doesn't come out much better in these illustrations of Dante's work. Purgatory is the most interesting place by far. In it are pictured weird monsters and plants. Light and darkness in peculiar shades and intensities. Beauty and ugliness existing together. You get the impression that in Purgatory you'll never know what's waiting around the next corner.

And that seems to fit more closely with what we know of God in this world. Nothing we do is either all one thing or all another. Our lives are mixtures of delight and sorrow, suffering and joy. In other words they are filled with challenge. Maybe Dante hasn't got all the truth. Who knows whether he's right or wrong about what the next life holds for us! But, if this life is anything to go by, whatever comes after it will probably offer just as much challenge and struggle as we face in our daily existence here and now. Because God will not take from us our capacity to make decisions for ourselves and order our actions according to definite choices we have made.

Almighty God, thank you for giving to us a world of challenge and decision. Help us to seek your will in all we do. Amen.

Disaster

A few times in each year we learn that there's been a big train crash or aeroplane disaster and that lots of people have been killed. When you think of the thousands of trains and aircraft which successfully and safely arrive at their destinations every day, the number of crashes is surprisingly small. But even one crash is one too many. How ought we to react when we hear that there's been an appalling accident like that involving the two Jumbo jets at Teneriffe in 1977?

Well we're not on hand so as far as helping out is concerned we can't do very much. Of course, Christians will pray for the survivors and all the injured. And ask God's blessing on the relations and friends of those who have been killed. Beyond these things there's not much we can do.

17

Even though air crashes are rare, every time there's really a bad one, people start saying that air liners shouldn't carry so many passengers. Or they ought not to try and land or take off in fog. All kinds of prescriptions to avoid future disasters are suggested. Pilots should fly less hours. Runways should be longer. More time should be allowed between one take off or landing and the next.

But when all reasonable precautions have been taken it remains true that accidents will happen. And in an age of advanced technical achievement the odd crash is the price we must pay for the thousands of quick, comfortable and safe journeys. This doesn't make the fact of the crash any more bearable especially for those who may have had relations and friends killed or injured. But it doesn't mean that we should adopt a negative attitude towards our technological achievements. While always insisting on the highest standards of safety, we must continue to have faith in our engineers and scientists, our aircrew and traffic control for they bring a world of great safety and convenience to us in more than ninety-nine percent of all cases.

Heavenly Father, we ask your gift of comfort to all who have lost relations or friends in rail and air crashes. Amen.

The Doctor's Decision

Very early in the twentieth century there lived a great man. A religious thinker who was also a medical doctor and a first class musician. His name was Albert Schweitzer. Perhaps his most famous book is *The Quest for the Historical Jesus*. Schweitzer tried for many years to show how faith in Jesus as the Son of God could be justified. But in *The Quest* he came to the reluctant conclusion that Jesus had been mistaken. That his error in thinking himself to be the Messiah was brought home to him horribly when he was dying on the cross. According to Schweitzer, this was when Jesus expected God to send angels to his aid and deliver him from that cruel death.

But there was no miraculous intervention on the first Good Friday and Jesus cried out 'My God, why have you forsaken me?' Then in pain and loneliness he died. It's not always easy to see just what Schweitzer makes of the resurrection. Enough to say that for him the game was up on Good Friday. He thought Jesus had been sadly mistaken and that was that. So Albert Schweitzer went off to a place called Lambarene in

Africa and built a hospital where he worked as doctor to the sick and the poor. No one would want to deny that this was a noble and generous act—giving up the quiet life of the scholar for the hectic and precarious existence of the jungle doctor.

But the great Swiss psychologist Carl Jung thinks Schweitzer was wrong. He should have stayed and battled with his New Testament studies because that was where his main gifts lay. Jung doesn't say that the jungle should have no doctors—only that a man who is first and foremost a brilliant theologian should regard his job of finding out about God to be of even greater importance.

Carl Jung reckons that what Schweitzer did in going to Lambarene was similar to a great doctor leaving his special practice to go and take church services for a handful of people. In other words, since there were other doctors, what Schweitzer did was a waste. You may not agree but at least there is a point here worth discussing.

Heavenly Father, teach us what you want us to do and give us strength to do it. Amen.

Early Light

The worst time of the year to have your birthday is near Christmas. Because friends and relations are apt to buy you just one present and make that do for both occasions. How much better to have a birthday in July or even in April so long as it's not on the first!

There's an ancient festival that comes just after Christmas and this too tends to be forgotten in our calendar. It's called Epiphany and occurs on the sixth of January. In a way you can't blame people for not making much of Epiphany—after all we're only just getting over the fun of plum pudding, turkey and first footing by then. But it's a pity we don't keep Epiphany as we might because it's a very cheerful festival.

To hold a feast at this time of year—when it's dark and cold and icy—is a custom which goes back long before the coming of Christianity. It used to be a great festival of lights. Bonfires and beacons would be lit to drive away the midwinter gloom and perhaps even offer a prayer to the sun god so that warm days might soon return.

Christians keep January sixth as the anniversary of the three kings' visit to Jesus, when they brought gold, frankincense and myrrh. You can look the story up in the second chapter of St. Matthew's gospel. Some

19

churches make a special event of it and hold a candle light service and perhaps a short children's drama of the presentation of the gifts to the Christ Child. A very cheerful thing to do in the dark of winter. It gets rid of that 'let down' feeling which often follows Christmas.

And there's a deeper message in it as well. It seems appropriate to celebrate the Epiphany with lights, for one of Christ's titles is Light of the World. In Matthew's story the three kings were wise enough to be guided to that light.

Heavenly Father, thank you for the comforts of lights and warmth in winter's darkness. Help us to lighten the lives of others. Amen.

Eastern Stargazers

Nearly every daily newspaper and all the magazines carry a section on the stars—your horoscope. It's amusing to while away a few minutes looking to see what the future has in store for you according to these charts. Provided of course that you don't take them too seriously. For when you come to think about it, twelve short paragraphs in a daily newspaper can't possible be accurate predictions for everybody. Not all Capricornians will go on a journey to a far country on the same day—or else the country would lose a twelfth of its population!

In the first Christmas story there's talk of stargazers or astrologers as they're sometimes called. These are the wise men mentioned in St. Matthew's Gospel who follow the Bethlehem Star to the birthplace of Jesus. It's said that they came from the east—the traditional place of astrologers. The place where foretelling the future from movements of the heavenly bodies was a well-established tradition.

Certainly in the time of Jesus many people believed in the astrologers' predictions. National leaders used to plan their warlike campaigns on evidence from these stargazers. They were the wise men of the ancient world. Matthew is wanting to tell us that the birth of Jesus was such an important event that the wisest and most expert men of the day came to pay homage to the Christ child.

It's a pretty story and a familiar part of the Christmas tradition. But what do we make of astrology nowadays? Can there be anything at all in the position of the stars which has to do with events on earth? Many would say not and answer that astrology is so much unscientific hocus pocus. But a growing number of people are thinking twice about the old saying 'What is above is below' meaning not that the stars cause events on earth but somehow their positions can coincide with what happens down here—provided you have the correct interpretation. It's food for thought.

Heavenly Father, thank you for the endless wonders of the universe. Help us never to become so set in our ways that we can't appreciate new ideas. Amen.

Eating Holiness

Have you ever wondered why we have parties? You might well reply, 'Because they're fun, that's why.' And true enough parties are where we get together with our friends and have a good time. But why is there such an emphasis on eating? A birthday party wouldn't be complete without sandwiches and sausage rolls. And where would Christmas be without the cake? Whenever human beings gather for a social occasion it seems they can't leave out food.

The same goes for religious festivals as well. In the Christian tradition alone we have Easter Eggs, Hot-Cross buns and Christmas cake. And most important of all there's the bread and wine of Holy Communion. In the New Testament we can read about Jesus breaking bread with his disciples in the upper room or eating fish with them beside the Sea of Galilee. Makes it all sound as if religion is one long feed!

In the Buddhist religion there's a saying 'He who eats by himself will keep his sin to himself.' It sounds very odd, threatening even. For who hasn't eaten by himself on some occasion or other? Perhaps Mum's in hospital and Dad's at work. You've got to eat by yourself then—or starve.

But this Buddhist saying isn't meant to be taken in such an absolutely straightforward way. It means rather something like the commandment to share—to show loving-kindness to others. And this is true not just of Buddhism but of Christianity, Judaism, Hinduism and all the other faiths. Each of them says that our full satisfaction and development as human beings and children of God is to be achieved only through sharing what we have with friends and strangers alike. If you're having a party soon, think of someone you weren't going to invite—then invite him.

Heavenly Father, all that we have comes from you. Help us to share. Amen.

The Eye of the Arrow Maker

An ancient Indian—not from the wild west but from India—went to visit an arrow maker. Probably so he could buy a new supply of weapons. The Indian's name was Janaka and he came from Benares.

Janaka had travelled a long way because arrow makers weren't to be found on every street corner. Manufacturing reliable weapons was a very skilled task and a long apprenticeship and training had to be served before you could set yourself up in business.

When Janaka arrived at the arrow maker's workshop he was surprised to see that the craftsman always kept one eye closed. He was told that this was so he could make absolutely sure with his other eye that the arrows he made were straight. After all, a crooked arrow is as bad as a broken bow. The arrow maker explained that if he kept both eyes open, then the things he saw through the eye he wasn't intentionally using interfered with his vision through the one needed for testing the straightness of the arrow. It's not all that different really from squinting or screwing up one eye in order to read small print in an English newspaper.

But behind both activities there's an interesting lesson to be drawn. In order to see one thing very clearly the viewer closes his vision to everything else which might distract. So if we really wish to achieve a particular success it's wise to concentrate on that aim and that alone. We can't do this all the time of course. But when we're playing a game, and we wish to play as well as we can, we should concentrate on all aspects of the game—fitness, training and skill. And the same is true in our work. Try it and see. Even the most difficult problems can be solved if we apply our full concentration to them.

Heavenly Father, help us to persevere in our work even when we find it very difficult. Amen.

Faith Over the Rainbow

There's an old tradition that if you find the end of a rainbow you'll discover a pot of gold there. The cases of people actually coming across gold in this way are very few in number—if indeed there are any. Perhaps the story arose in the first place out of the obvious beauty and strangeness of rainbows. We don't see rainbows every day. There's something magical about the way they appear at the height of a rainstorm and add marvellous colours to the scene. Something so enchanting and surprising that you could almost believe that great riches were to be found at the exact point where this bow of the sky meets the earth's wet greenness.

And then a pot of gold is a happy ending in more ways than one. Often the rain comes and spoils our plans for a picnic or a game of cricket. It's a compensation for ruined pleasure to imagine that the rainbow is a magical bringer of wealth.

Some people have the sort of faith in God which we associate with rainbows and pots of gold. They don't really take God seriously but think of him as a kind of fantasy—just like magical coins in the rain. And they suggest that having faith in God is a rather pleasant and charming but utterly fanciful thing like expecting to find pots of gold at a rainbow's end. As if God doesn't really belong to ordinary everyday life but acts like a Father Christmas of the imagination.

The ancient people who wrote the Bible knew better, and this is shown in the Old Testament story of the rainbow after the flood. For them it was a sign that God is someone who can always be trusted—not just on special occasions and in particular places. And that's still true. God doesn't come and go like rainbows and spring showers. He cares for us all the time.

Heavenly Father, help us to see your presence in the wonders of nature and give us a lasting trust in your love for us. Amen.

Fear Itself

Nearly everybody has dreamed that horrid dream of being chased up and down stairs, over river bridges and to the tops of tall buildings. It doesn't matter that you don't know who's chasing you or what he might do when he catches up. The only desperately important thing is not to be caught. It's a kind of worry and terror dream—a nightmare. And far more frightening than all the monsters from space and from under the sea put together. It's the fear of the unknown. The fear of 'I-don't-know-what'.

A writer called Franz Kafka wrote a story in which the hero is to go on trial. He's not up for theft or murder or anything like that. The terror of Kafka's story comes from the fact that the hero isn't even told why he's being tried. And he's not allowed to know the identity of his accusers.

Both Kafka and whatever makes us dream of being chased by unknown monsters are on to the truth that it's fear of the unknown and the unseen which terrifies us most. If you're being chased by a lion that's frightening enough. But at least you know the power of the pursuer—and more important still, what will stop him in his tracks—a shot from the hunter. But fear of a ghost or the dark or an unseen enemy is the very worst kind of terror.

However, there is a cure for it. And that cure is something the New Testament asks us to take. It's the cure of faith. When our nightly dreams and fears spill over into the day and make us anxious we should try and remember that whatever is causing our fear—even when we don't know what it is—is under the control of God. We needn't be afraid to trust his world for even the unknown is known to God.

Heavenly Father, help us when we are afraid; when we have nightmares; when we're alone and unable to sleep. Amen.

Flying Saucers

In the old days people believed that the earth was flat and that the sky stretched above it like a curved blue skin. And they thought that the rain came through little holes in this blue roof. Far above the sky was heaven where God lived with his angels.

This God sometimes sent messengers to visit the earth and intervene in the affairs of mankind. And the people believed that on a day in the future the world would end and the God who lived above the sky would sit and judge all the men and women who had lived on earth.

Then, so the story goes, mankind grew up and discovered that the world wasn't flat but round. And they learned that there was after all no sky-god. And they made rockets and sputniks and space ships. They visited the moon and took pictures to prove they'd been there.

But the funny thing was that the same men and women liked to read about flying saucers—visitors from other civilisations deep in space. Some even said they'd seen flying saucers for themselves. That they'd had messages from the visitors who came out of the sky and these visitors had warned of strange and terrible happenings which were yet to come.

Then one person stood up and said, 'What's the difference between the old stories about gods and angels above the curved blue ceiling and your belief in a super intelligent civilisation from outer space which visits us in saucer shaped spaceships?'

Is it true that there's something about us which always looks outside ourselves and even outside the known world for help? And if this is true, why do we do so? Could flying saucers be the old gods in a new form?

Heavenly Father, teach us not to close our minds to new visions and not to laugh at old truths. Amen.

The Force of *Star Wars*

Early in 1978 a new craze swept all over the land. All the commotion was caused by a new film from America called *Star Wars*. You'd hardly believe that a mere film could have such an effect. But thousands and thousands of people queued to see it. Not just young folk either but grown men and women, grannies and grandads even. You could wait for hours outside the cinema in Leicester Square just to get a ticket. And not even one for the next performance but for the same show the week after next!

Surely it must have been a great film to attract so much attention? And yet many people were disappointed by it. The story was quite interesting but like so many we'd heard before. The goodies—a fine young man and a beautiful princess fighting against the powers of evil and destruction: dark and ugly men in a sinister spaceship.

Some of the special affects were outstanding. Especially the two robots which were almost human. Well—one of them was at any rate. The other was like a cheeky domestic pet. A bit like Dr. Who's K.9. but bigger of course. There was a wise old man too. Like Merlin or a magician from one of Grimm's fairy tales. And the battles were noisy and exciting. Somehow the film makers had even got God into the adventure—though they didn't call him God but 'The Force' instead. In fact the goodies kept saying 'May the Force be with you' just as a priest might say 'The Lord be with you' or 'May God Bless you' in an ordinary church service.

But for all these things—and the ending which shouldn't be given away—*Star Wars* was a bit of a let down to quite a lot of people. Is this because we're beginning at last to get tired of the slogans 'terrific, spectacular' and 'bigger and better'? Down the road from Leicester Square they were showing a Disney cartoon in a small local cinema. It was playing to packed houses. What can we learn from that?

Heavenly Father, help us not to crave all the time for more and more spectacular entertainments. Let us not forget the enjoyment in a quiet tale well told. Amen.

A Future Hope

On Easter Day, Jesus rose from the dead. You might wonder just what this can mean. Are we really expected to believe in this age of science that a dead man came back from the grave? It sounds impossible. Surely we now know that there's no heaven in the sky. Gods and devils are only for primitive people to believe in. And when you're dead, well straightforward and unromantic it may sound but, that's all there is to it. Our bodies die and pass into the ground and that's the end of the matter.

All this might well be true. But, just in case we're tempted to believe everything that anybody claims because it's supposed to be 'scientific' we'll do well to remember that the way of thought which we associate with science is only a few hundred years old. Perhaps our tidy minded way of looking at the world isn't the whole story. Shakespeare has one of the characters in 'Hamlet' say 'There are more things in heaven and earth than are dreamed of in your philosophy.' It's not certain by any means that twentieth century thinking can tell us everything about the world. Perhaps, in some way as yet unknown to us, the dead might be raised. Maybe death isn't the end of all life. We're in no position to make dogmatic statements.

But the truth about the resurrection of Jesus doesn't depend upon whether people rise from the dead or not. To find the meaning of Easter we need to go back to Good Friday—to the crucifixion. On that day Jesus' friends and disciples were scattered about the land in fear of the authorities—scared in case the same thing should happen to them. After the resurrection they became unafraid, confident and filled with hope.

Now if Jesus didn't rise from the dead, something equally amazing must have happened to fill them with such courage and hope. And that's at least one meaning of Easter—hope. A sign that no matter how bleak and empty life becomes, there's always room for a hope for the future.

Heavenly Father, we see what a great mystery is the resurrection on the first Easter Day. Give us that same confidence and hope for the future which was shared by the first disciples. Amen.

The German Measles Party

Nobody enjoys catching diseases. A day off school with a sore throat isn't all that bad—if you like lemon juice nice and hot and if there's a good play or your kind of pop music on the radio. But serious illness is a different matter altogether. In the Middle Ages millions died of the plague. Only sixty years ago influenza was a killer. Measles—joked about as dotty and spotty in the weekly comics—was a very serious disease not so long ago. Certainly one you'd try to avoid catching.

In fact thanks to all the vitamins and antibiotics we've got nowadays it's possible to avoid catching many of the diseases which were once so greatly feared. Food is kept under more hygienic conditions. Housing is better. All these things help to improve the state of our health.

So how surprising to hear of a group of children getting together with the deliberate idea of becoming ill. Holding a party simply to fall sick! Not through eating too much trifle or too many cream buns but by coming into contact with someone who has a foreign sounding sickness—German Measles.

But there's method in this madness. You see German Measles isn't usually a very serious illness. A few spots. A slight temperature. And an itch at the back of the neck. Not much to worry about. Except if grown women catch German Measles when they're expecting a baby it can have serious effects. Not on the woman herself but on her baby which may be born with a severe handicap.

But if she's had German Measles already as a child then it's extremely unlikely that she'll catch it again when she's grown up—when it's most dangerous. This is an obvious example of someone suffering so that someone else does not suffer more severely later on. It's also a nice comfort to know that some nasty things—like diseases can only be caught once. And that we're able to put illness in a humorous perspective and beat it at the same time—at a party.

Heavenly Father, thank you for doctors and nurses. For all who care for the sick. Help us to be strong and cheerful when we're ill. Amen.

Giovanni's Principle

If you could combine a theory about ghosts and hell with the best tunes ever written you'd have a smash hit. That's what Mozart did in his opera *Don Giovanni* almost two hundred years ago. There's a lot more to it than that but if you like violent endings then this opera might be just the thing for you.

It's about a nobleman called by the same name as the opera itself—Don Giovanni. His sole occupations in life are eating, drinking and captivating young ladies. One such young lady Donna Anna, is the daughter of a high ranking officer—The Commandant. When he appears on the scene to protect his daughter, Don Giovanni kills him with his sword and continues conscienceless in his bad ways almost to the end of the story.

Eventually a statue is erected to the Commandant's memory and one night in the graveyard the unrepentant Don Giovanni invites it to supper. Now in fairy tales and operas, all kinds of impossible things can happen. And so the statue accepts the offer to dine out. Mozart composed some of his most terrifying music for the statue's entrance to Giovanni's banqueting hall. He comes of course for revenge. But the great womanizer refuses to repent so is taken by the Commandant's ghost to where the fires of hell await him.

Then the opera is all over except for a final chorus where all the well behaved people sing in delight at the Don's downfall: 'So perish all rogues'. Really that last chorus is Mozart's laugh at his audience. He's saying something like: 'Don Giovanni went to hell for a *principle* even if it wasn't a desirable principle. You lot are so fickle and weak you don't have any real principles'. So called 'polite society' in the late eighteenth century didn't even realise Mozart was making fun of them.

No one wants to suggest that Don Giovanni was a good man—an example to be followed—except in *one* respect: He was a man of his word. He was absolutely consistent. May this be said of us: 'He or she was a person to be trusted.'

Heavenly Father, help us to think generously before we promise; then give us grace to keep our promises. Amen.

God in Disguise?

In a small Yorkshire town—Wetherby perhaps—there's a woman who dresses very oddly. At least she looks odd. Not her but her clothes you understand. In fact you can't see much of her at all because of the clothes. She wears a long dress like an Indian sari and a full length cloak. Sandals on her feet and extra large sun glasses hiding the eyes. Her hair is cut in curls like Tom Baker who sometimes plays 'Dr. Who.'

If you saw this lady you'd be tempted to say she was in disguise—especially the cloak and sun glasses part. They make her look like a spy or a secret agent. But it's all a bit ridiculous really when you think about it. Her unusual clothing makes her stand out in the crowd so it isn't an effective disguise at all. Mind you, she probably doesn't intend to conceal her identity. It's just the way she chooses to dress. But if she did want to go unnoticed it would be the wrong way of going about it—wearing such extravagant clothing. That's why disguise outfits that young children often buy are so funny. They don't disguise you—they make you look even more obvious.

But the idea of disguises isn't just limited to women in Wetherby, to secret agents or to mischievous children. It gets in everywhere—even into hymns. There's a line in a hymn by Wesley. It's about Jesus and it says 'Veiled in flesh the godhead see.' You may know it's part of *Hark the Herald Angels.'* We sing it at Christmas. And the trouble with that line is it suggests Jesus was not really a man at all. It says that while he might look like a man he was really God dressed up all the time. God in disguise.

And that's not a very Christian belief because the New Testament tells us that in some mysterious way Jesus was man *and* God—not God pretending to be a man, disguised as a man. Only by really becoming a man like us could God understand our human condition. And that is a very long and glorious story. It begins with the Christmas hymns.

Heavenly Father, thank you for becoming a human being like us at the first Christmas. For understanding us and for loving us. Amen.

God in Space

When the Russians sent a rocket into space in the 1960's the world heard by radio from its pilot that 'We haven't seen God up here.' This was meant as a joke against believers in the West. For the Russians live in a communist state and they don't believe in God.

It may be that there are a few exceedingly simple people who still think God lives in the sky—in other words that he's the sort of being you could get to see in a space rocket. But most Christians, indeed most believers of any faith, wouldn't want to say that God makes his home above the clouds.

The idea of heaven in the sky dates from a much earlier time when people thought that the earth was the centre of the universe and that God lived in a heaven above the waters that were supposed to be above the world.

Ever since the astronomer Copernicus we've all known that our planet is in fact but one part of our sun's area of space—our solar system as it's called. And that geographically we're not half so important as we once thought we were.

Of course the Russian cosmonauts' jibe is quite empty. He shouldn't have expected to see God with the naked eye out in space any more than he would fancy his chances of meeting him in that way down here on earth. For God isn't a solid substance or a ghost but a spiritual being. He doesn't play tricks on us like the invisible man. And he doesn't hide himself away in space either.

He does show us how we can communicate with him though. And that's by prayer in faith. Even this doesn't mean we're to be down on our knees all the time making every day like Sunday. It does mean that wherever we go in the world, even if like the Russian cosmonaut we venture into space, we're still able to reckon on God's love and care.

Heavenly Father, thank you for the sun, the moon and the stars, for the wonder of travel in space. Give us the gift of faith so that wherever we are we may feel confident in calling on your name. Amen.

'And God Reckoned...'

How would you like a career in accountacy? Maybe it's not as bad as you think. Not simply adding up columns of figures or trying to find out where all the company spends its cash. But perhaps an accountant for a firm that makes products you're interested in. An aircraft company or a chocolate factory. Even football clubs need accountants.

Of course you would actually need to be able to add up properly. No use having an accountant in the company if the boss has to hire another one to check all his totals. You'd end up having an army of accountants that way.

And you would have to see that the receipts and payments balanced. That means you'd look for cheques paying all the company's debts and for more cheques in payment for services and goods provided by your organisation. This would all have to be very neat, tidy and accurate.

Some people think of God as if he's a sort of spiritual accountant. Someone who takes careful note of all our good deeds and our bad deeds and weighs or balances them against each other. If the good deeds weigh heavier—because there are more of them—then you find favour in God's eyes. But if the bad deeds weigh heavier... Oh dear! It's 'down below' you go!

Well *some* people think like this but it's not the way the Bible pictures God. In the first book of the Bible called 'Genesis' it says that 'Abraham believed in God and God reckoned that as righteousness'—'justice', if you like. Now that sort of God wouldn't get a job as an accountant would he? What has believing to do with justice and being good? But that's the way the God of Jews and Christians works. He doesn't carefully weigh every sin—as Ebenezer Scrooge might count pennies—and then punish accordingly. He looks at what we believe and reckons our belief or as it sometimes says in the Bible 'faith' and measures us on that basis. Well, what do you believe?

Heavenly Father, we thank you for loving us and for showing your love to people like Abraham. Help us to understand more clearly what you are like. Amen.

The Googol

It's odd that when we refer to numbers of objects we say, 'One', 'Two', 'Three' etc and then 'A few', 'Several', 'A lot' and 'Many'. Numbers only have special names up to ten and then it's all repetitions. 'Twenty-one', 'Thirty-one' and so on. Not until 'A hundred' is there a significant new name. And then you've to wait for 'A thousand' through all the boring hundreds of thousands to 'A million'. Through the thousands of millions to 'A billion'.

It's interesting to find that beyond the million and the billion there's another number with a strange sounding name—the Googol. What a marvellous sound. Like something that's part flower and part frog. And yet there it is in the mathematical textbooks—the Googol. Even beyond the Googol there's another bigger number—the Googoloplex. And this one's so big that the mathematicians say there are more units in the Googoloplex than there are atoms in the universe! For a Googoloplex is a Googol multiplied by a Googol.

From a religious point of view the Googol and its big brother have great significance. You might not think it. After all, what's a number—just an anonymous pause in the process of counting. But there's more to it than that. The fact that people have taken the trouble to give a name to an extremely large and scarcely used number shows that we have some respect for the individual and personal qualitites—even in large scale arithmetic. You often hear it said 'We're only numbers in a book or on computer tape'. But numbers, or so it seems, aren't *just* numbers after all. Even the largest has a name, and a strange pantomime name at that. Perhaps this is because the created universe isn't simply a machine but it shares in the personality of the God who made it.

Almighty God, teach us to respect life and personality and help us never to treat people as if they were machines. Amen.

Gorky in the Graveyard

When school is finished for good, for ever—yes when that great day dawns—some young people take up what's called an apprenticeship. This means they go and work for a craftsman, perhaps a plumber or an engineer, and learn the trade while they're working. Learning by experience. The same goes for those who train to be doctors, nurses, dentists or lawyers. It's always necessary to add practical experience to book learning.

A Russian writer called Maxim Gorky wrote a book about his apprenticeship—about his life from about the age of eleven onwards. He tells of all the experiences which eventually helped him to become a writer. And there's a truth—writers need apprenticeships too. You can't write about nothing. The best writers are often those who have had lots of different experiences.

Now whatever you decide to do it's an added bonus if you find your apprenticeship enjoyable. Work isn't always fun, but certain aspects of it sometimes can be—like taking a pride in what you make and being given credit for what you've done.

In Gorky's strange apprenticeship he was once dared to sleep on a gravetop in the cemetry. He went there as it began to get dark and lay down all alone. As it got later he grew more and more scared. And the howls from cats together with the human catcalls of his friends didn't help much either. Besides it was cold and very, very dark. Then it became absolutely silent and stayed that way for what seemed hours.

But Gorky made it and won his bet. He stayed on the gravetop all night. The trouble was he didn't get the credit for his dare. All his friends said they'd known all the time that there weren't such things as ghosts and anyone could do what Gorky did. But they weren't in any rush to do it themselves! There's something true about this that's not just to do with graves in the dead of night. It's that we have to live knowing that sometimes we won't always get the praise we think we deserve.

Heavenly Father, help us always to praise where praise is due and to work well without thought of reward. Amen.

Harvest of the Spirit

In the country, harvest festival is still a very important time in the year. That's because there people are close to nature. They can see easily just how much we depend on the produce of the ground. In towns it's not so simple. Some people in the middle of our suburbs have never even seen a cow. And lamposts are more common than trees.

Here it's a good idea to call industry to mind. The work done in our offices and factories is also vital to our way of life. So townspeople can celebrate the harvest festival just as realistically as those who live in the wide open spaces.

Harvest is an ancient festival. Much older than the church and the christian faith. In fact older than all the great religions of the world. And it is so old precisely because of its importance. A feast connected with food must be one of the most basic feasts it's possible to have. For without food we'd all be dead. Primitive people knew this well, and that's why they observed harvest as a religious occasion.

When we get behind the corn, the banana skins and the local autumn fair and dance, what can we say about harvest which is true not just for ancient people but for all time?

We can see that in the harvest man brings his individual personal energy to bear upon the world of nature. And it doesn't need much imagination to move from that to the realisation that, not just in the autumn but in all seasons, human beings at their best are able to affect and change the natural order. And that they do so by the operation of creative minds and limbs. So in a sense all the year round is harvest, because in every month men and women act creatively upon the raw material of the world.

Heavenly Father, thank you for all that there is. Help us to work closely with your purposes so that the world may be enriched. Amen.

The Head Of Peter Tchaikovsky

There are lots of superstitious people in the world—at least judging by the numbers who read their 'stars' every day in the newspapers. Then there's not walking under ladders, throwing a pinch of spilled salt over your shoulder. That's done because the devil is supposed to like salt, so if you spill any he'll creep up behind you. Just the time to let him have it—right in the eye!

Apart from common superstitions like these there are other odd beliefs which are illnesses in a way. Psychologists and Psychiatrists have even given them medical names. Don't you like going in lifts or any sort of closed space? 'Ah,' they'll say, 'you've got claustrophobia.' The opposite of that is agoraphobia—fear of wide open places. And Xeno-phobia, terror at the prospect of coming across anything unknown.

There's no end to the number of these complaints. Really they're just long latin or greek words for whatever you're afraid of and then the word 'phobia' meaning 'fear' is tacked on the end. You can have icthyophobia if you like—fear of fishes.

The composer of *The 1812 Overture*—the piece with all the cannon fire in it, often heard played by the Hollywood Bowl Symphony Orchestra—had a very strange fear. He was called Peter Tchaikovsky and he lived in terror that his head would fall off. He even used to go around with one arm raised to his chin as if to keep it on.

Now it's very easy to laugh at poor old Tchaikovsky—or at least at his strange idea of the falling head. But these strange and unreasonable fears can afflict anyone and often cause a great amount of suffering. They are difficult to cure, because it's hard to see exactly what causes them. It's clear they're mental rather than physical illnesses. But they're no less disabling for that.

Almighty Father, be with us when we are afraid. And especially when we're still afraid even when we've been assured that there's nothing to be afraid of. Amen.

Hell Fire and Damnation

Think of the most horrid torture you can imagine. It may be having your feet tickled by feathers or your eyes slowly put out by red hot needles. There's not much chance that anything of the kind will ever happen to you of course. Perhaps that's why such frightening events have a fatal fascination for us like horror films or ghost stories.

But little more than a hundred years ago many church people believed that sinners when they died went straight to hell. And in hell they suffered horrible punishments, not just for a day or a week but for ever. A few clergymen got together and, so disgusted were they at this thought that they produced a book which said that nothing of the kind happened after death. The book was called *Essays and Reviews*.

Still some so called Christians insisted on believing in eternal torment and actually brought the authors of *Essays and Reviews* to trial in the church courts. Amazingly the writers were found guilty. But they appealed to the House of Lords and eventually they were acquitted. At this trial a wit remarked that the Lord Chancellor had 'dismissed hell with costs and taken away from orthodox members of the Church of England their last hope of everlasting damnation.'

One defence of the authors of *Essays and Reviews* was that everlasting punishment gave men no hope of forgiveness, no hope for the future. And it was argued, no God of love, such as we see in the stories about Jesus, would ever leave those whom he'd created without hope.

These days people don't worry too much about heaven and hell. But the writers of *Essays and Reviews* still have a point. No matter how bad things get we must never regard our lives as hopeless because God never leaves us without some possibility in the future. We should remember that when things seem very black.

Heavenly Father, help us always to hope even when everything seems dark and worrying. Help us to trust in your goodness and to find peace in doing your will. Amen.

Hollywood Religion

Easter is a time when film makers get their biggest audiences. It's a time for showing off religious epics about the life of Jesus such as *The Greatest Story Ever Told* and *Jesus of Nazareth*. Perhaps it's a good thing for the films and television to find a place for God at Easter. And many religious or biblical films are colourful and exciting.

You know the kind of thing: Angels with golden wings, voices from heaven. Earthquakes. Clouds. The parting of the Red Sea and many more celluloid miracles. All very dramatic and most entertaining.

But the trouble with spectacular films about God and religion is that they so easily give rise to misleading impressions about the nature of the world and God's purpose for us. For instance, we don't see many angels descending from heaven these days. And the idea of someone rising from the grave doesn't seem to be one that's rooted in everyday experience. Stories of miraculous cures can be cruel even—especially if someone near to you is suffering from a serious illness. Why doesn't God heal them with one of his miracles—like he seems to have done so often in the past if religious films are anything to go by?

The main problem with biblical epics on the screen is that by portraying God as one who acts dramatically in the world they frequently suggest that that's the only way he acts. So that we lose heart if our prayers aren't followed by instant miracles.

The fact is that God sometimes does act dramatically but more often his relationship with the world is more down to earth and ordinary. For example, human beings instead of angels regularly carry messages of hope and doctors and nurses bring about the cure and relief of sick people. These unsensational events would never make exciting films but they're the work of God just the same.

Heavenly Father, teach us to appreciate your involvement in ordinary things. Amen.

Hunger

'You can't talk about the feeding of the five thousand when there's a Wimpy Bar on every corner.' It's a problem isn't it? How do we interpret that story to a nation that's well fed—overfed even? But we've all known what it's like to be really hungry even if only for a short time. Perhaps after an illness. Maybe through going without food deliberately say on Good Friday and sending the money you've saved to Oxfam or Christian Aid. Luckily for most of us the problem of real hunger over a prolonged period doesn't arise—it does for many people in India and South America. And it did for a lot of folks in our own country during the last century.

No doubt you've come across books like *Oliver Twist* by Charles Dickens and Kingsley's *Water Babies*. These were written partly to draw attention to the hideous facts of starvation and malnutrition. Perhaps you've heard of Christians like Stuart Headlam who supported the movement to bring a better diet to the poor in the large industrial towns? There was—and still is—the Salvation Army.

A novelist called Knut Hamsun wrote a book called *Hunger*. You might expect it to deal with the condition of the poor in the same way that Dickens and Kingsley did. But not at all. Hamsun's book is quite different. He sets out to show that as well as physical hunger there's a hunger in the mind and spirit for lively ideas and imaginative stories.

You might ask, 'What's the use of a work of fiction to a starving man?' And perhaps the answer is 'Very little.' But there's another question, 'What's the point in feeding a man if afterwards he's still as dull and unthinking as a robot?' Mechanical men—even mechanical men with full stomachs—are boring. Knut Hamsun is trying to tell us that we need the life of the mind as well as food for the body. Jesus said the same thing: 'You shall not live by bread alone.'

Heavenly Father, teach us to concern ourselves with providing food for the hungry and a fair share of the world's riches for all men. And help us not to neglect the needs of our mind and spirit. Amen

Immanuel (Punctual) Kant

If you've ever been late for school you'll have been told all about punctuality. The importance of arriving in good time. But sometimes no matter how hard we try we are late. The bus breaks down. Or there's a long hold up because a sugar tanker spills its load right across the main street. Even if you have an electric alarm it can let you down when there's a power cut.

Now punctuality was something that the philosopher Immanuel Kant knew all about. In fact it's said that the townspeople in the small town where he lived could set their watches by him. Every morning at exactly eleven o'clock he set off from his home to the coffee house.

Well it's easy to be on time if you don't have to be anywhere until eleven o'clock. Maybe there'd be more point in Mr Kant boasting about his punctuality if he'd set off for the coffee house nice and early—say about eight in the morning. About the time we're starting out for school.

That's fair comment really. But the useful lesson to be drawn from Kant's good timekeeping isn't much to do with the virtues of getting up early as with the regularity of his daily appearance. The villagers could set their watches by him. We all depend on regularities of a different kind. Such as morning following night and spring after winter. We take on trust the regular workings of gravity. It'd be a strange and worrying world where breakfasts floated off the table into the air just as we were about to eat! Some people think that the existence of order and regularity in the world is a sign of God's existence. But whether God exists or not, all our scientific and everyday knowledge is based on our taking for granted the continuance of a regular sequence of events.

Heavenly Father, teach us to look at the world and to wonder. Amen.

38

The Invisible Choir

In pantomime and opera everyone likes the main characters. The Prince Charming. The beautiful princess. The King. The fair maiden. Even the wicked witch or the Queen of the Night gets the occasional hiss. Not even the frog is left out. It's understandable really for these are on the stage for the biggest part of the action. And they have the most exciting tasks to perform, the most interesting words to say.

In the end the prince marries his princess and the wicked witch is banished into outer darkness. But that's not the whole of the story. Operas and pantomimes include people who are the chorus or the choir. It's their job to describe the action and add colour and variety to the plot. To provide background.

And their job doesn't stop there. Something much more important is included in their task. The choir often comforts and advises the hero and heroine. In the *Magic Flute* for instance when Tamino thinks he's lost his love for ever the chorus answers him 'Pamina', that's his girl friend, 'Pamina is still alive'. Now being in the choir isn't a prominent part. It means taking a minor role, of being in the background. Sometimes even off stage and out of sight. George Eliot has written a poem about these helpers who are important even if they can't be seen. The poem's called *The Choir Invisible* and it's job according to George Eliot is to be strength to people in agony and distress.

We can move right off the stage and into real life now. For to be part of an invisible body of human beings who are always ready to help others is what we're all called to be. Not always at the front of the stage but necessary just the same.

Heavenly Father, help us to offer strength to other people when they ask for our support. Amen.

Inwardly Digest

There's a marvellously funny book called *The Heart of a Dog* and it's written by Mikhail Bulgakov. It chapter two it says: 'There are forty thousand dogs in Moscow and I'll bet there's not one of them so stupid he can't spell out the word 'sausage'. The whole book is about a dog—a dog who's changed into a man (or something like a man) in a scientific experiment. Very improbable no doubt but highly amusing reading.

But why does Bulgakov say that all dogs can spell 'sausage'? Surely he doesn't mean to suggest they can really read! Otherwise why can't they read 'Keep off the grass'? No the point is that we humans read what we like to read just as a dog, if suddenly blessed with special powers, would read 'sausage'—because *he* likes sausage.

This goes for all kinds of books and magazines. Many a teenager would rather read a weekly paper about pop music than pick up the *Financial Times*. And who's to blame him? Adults read about their special hobbies. 'What's dad reading?' 'Oh just another gardening book that's all.' He reads what he likes. We all read what we like and tend to leave the rest. But to get back to Bulgakov's dog for a minute: He can read 'sausage' because sausages are a luxury food for dogs. Just look how we use words to do with eating for talking about what we read.

How often we say 'I can't swallow that' of some weird story or other. There's even a magazine called *Reader's Digest*. And we say of some books that they're *dry*—almost as if we can taste them and they don't taste too good. The English Prayer Book uses the idea of food and digestion in a prayer about the Bible stories 'Grant', it says 'that we may read, mark, learn and inwardly digest them . . .' It doesn't mean eating Bibles any more than Bulgakov thinks dogs can read sausages. It does mean reading with a good appetite—an appetite for knowledge.

Heavenly Father, teach us to read with enthusiasm and help us particularly when we find our lessons hard. Amen.

Is God Dead?

Some people think that religion is for old ladies and young kids. A kind of fairy story that's a comfort to children in the dark but which gets forgotten as soon as they leave Sunday School. Or that belief in God is a sort of fire insurance which old people take out just in case.

It makes you think whether perhaps religion is for weak and immature people but has no value for grown up men and women who can stand on their own feet. Maybe we should give up using God as a prop—someone to call upon when we're afraid or in need of comfort.

In the last century a man called Nietzsche wrote a book in which he said 'God is Dead!' It caused a great stir among religious people who called him an atheist and a blasphemer. What kind of statement is that—'God is Dead'? Did Nietzsche really mean to tell us that the creator of the universe had died? Perhaps he just meant that there never has been a God. That the universe doesn't need a supernatural being in order to account for its existence and that men and women should take responsibility for their own actions and not look to God all the time.

What can Christians make of the idea that God is Dead? Perhaps that some of us hold very childish ideas about God. That he's an old man in the sky or that he'll work miracles every five minutes to get us out of our difficulties. There's no doubt that these selfish and silly ideas about God should die. Our image of God must grow. But if the experience of thousands of Christians is anything to go by God shows by answering prayers in his own time and in his own way that he's not dead at all but very much alive.

Heavenly Father, give us a mature faith and wisdom to understand your ways in the world. Amen.

Is God pleased?

There's a kind of cartoon or caricature of God that suggests he's an old man who lives above the sky. And he's a very grumpy old man and hard to please. He waits night and morning for prayers and complains if he doesn't get them. Perhaps that's what the thunder is? He counts the empty pews in church and feels angry. This God watches to see if anyone is going to break one of his rules. When we do he gets annoyed.

Of course, God isn't really like this at all. He's not a grumpy old grandad in the sky. So what is he like then? Some people talk about God in words which describe him as a Life Force or as the Cause of all things. Others say God is the Absolute—whatever that might mean— and they give the Absolute a capital 'A'.

Well perhaps God is Life Force, Cause and Absolute all three and many more things besides. But those words make him seem to be very remote—as if he's the unseen head of a government department. And no doubt it's impossible to believe in the grumpy grandad God—the Old Man in the Sky. But at least that kind of God is more interesting than the civil service version called The Absolute. A section from the church's Prayer Book doesn't make God seem very personal either when it describes him as 'without body, parts or passions.'

But the Bible tells us of quite a different God. God who is personal enough to wrestle with Jacob. To argue with Abraham. And to be angry with Moses. These are stories of course—legends or parables if you like. But they convey a meaning and that is thàt God wants us to think of him as a person and not as an object.

The New Testament part of the Bible goes even further when Jesus teaches us to call God 'Father'. Not the mechanical absolute but a person who loves us. The Collect—that's a special prayer—for the first Sunday after Trinity talks about human beings *pleasing* God. That's a good thought. God is no caricature. But he's not a machine either. He is pleased when we return his love for us by loving one another.

> Father in Heaven help us to love one another as you have first loved us. Amen.

It never rains at Camberwick Green

In between the test match and the early news you can see the television programme for young children—*Camberwick Green*. It's a marvellous programme. You should watch it next time you get the chance in the school holidays. And it's a wonderful place Camberwick Green. Everything goes like clockwork there.

Mickey Murphy's loaves always come out on time well baked. Windy Miller never gets hit by the sails of his windmill as he dodges in and out—even when he's been at the cider. Lord Bellborough's train runs on time. And, when the gentle day's work is done, there's the regular band concert. It's all free and it never rains.

You could think of Camberwick Green as heaven. No trouble. No homework. No rush or fuss and bother. And the sun always shines. We know that life's not like this at all—not real life. Almost every day something goes wrong. You lose your pen. It rains and spoils the cricket match. You go down with flu on your birthday. When it snows you find your boots leak. Camberwick Green's ideal world is unbelievable. That's why older children don't watch it much. It's not meant for us. It's childish. O.K. for the tots who are just beginning to learn the English language but as we get older we put away childish things.

Now although the way they live in Camberwick Green is so unreal many people try to make their own lives like life in that animated village. Smooth. Easy. Trouble-free. The television advertisements encourage us to do this by their silly claims that if only we use this or that toothpaste, this or that shampoo life will be an endless comfortable dream.

It'll never be like that in this world. But perhaps it will in heaven? Angels, harps and all that. Like Camberwick Green only better. It's not likely, because God always seems to have something important for us to do. Something that's worth doing—even if it's a struggle. God has arranged things so that we develop through struggle. God has arranged things so that we develop through struggle. Let us not refuse the challenge and tell him we'd rather live in a cartoon village where it never rains instead.

Heavenly Father, help us when life seems to be a very heavy struggle. Amen.

It's Not Cricket

In the Second Test Match on England's tour of New Zealand in 1978 an English batsman was run out. Nothing unusual about that—players are dismissed in this way all the time. But it was the *way* Derek Randall was run out which caused all the fuss. He was backing up when the New Zealand bowler Chatfield whipped off the bails at the end of his run up and appealed for a run out. Randall was out of his ground looking for the chance of a quick single, and so he was out.

Now *all* batsmen back up. They're taught to do it from the earliest days of coaching. But it is a dangerous game and can get you run out. The point is though that it's customary for the bowler to give a warning: 'If you do that again, I'll run you out.' He doesn't have to give a warning, but it's the custom, the 'done thing', the sporting and gentlemanly way to play the game. Chatfield was acting within the laws of the game but not in the spirit of cricket.

He should have let Randall off with a warning. It's all a bit like something that happened in the New Testament. Simon Peter asks Jesus how many times he should forgive someone who's been offensive. Peter was a bit more generous than the New Zealander though—more generous than any bowler could afford to be. He said, 'Should I forgive him as many as seven times?' Jesus said 'Not seven times but seventy times seven.' And he meant by this that Peter should *always* forgive.

This is very similar to what happened in that Test Match—played in Christchurch oddly enough. In both cases the law said one thing but the spirit said something else. We need laws in this far from perfect world. But when we try to justify our every action in terms of law like the bowler, like Peter who wanted a definite ruling, then we lose the spirit of living altogether. We all do it and we're usually sorry afterwards. One paper said Chatfield apologised—that he was sorry too.

Heavenly Father, give us a forgiving spirit and help us not to bear grudges against those who do wrong to us. Amen.

Land of Hope and Elgar

It must be awful to write a tune that you're not all that keen on and find that it's played wherever you go. Something similar happened to the composer Edward Elgar. He invented a tune called *Pomp and Circumstance* and somebody went and put to it the familiar words:

'Land of Hope and Glory, Mother of the free.
How shall we extol thee who are born of thee?'

This is a particular song of course. One which tries to encourage us to have pride in our country and sometimes unfortunately to be enthusiastic about killing people who don't agree with our foreign policy. No wonder that Elgar became tired of hearing his tune when it was associated with a militaristic and warlike attitude.

But the writer G. K. Chesterton showed that love of one's country—'patriotism' as it's called needn't always mean 'my country right or wrong'. In fact Chesterton said that the true patriot might even be the man who criticises his country most. The writer who makes fun of Britain might well be the man who loves it best. And this, he claimed, is true because when we have a good look at everything said and done in the name of our country we're forced to admit that some of those things are far from good.

Then, says Chesterton, the one who really loves his country—the true patriot will speak out against evil and injustice so that the country he loves may become worthy of that love. This idea doesn't just apply to nations but to all groups of people. A football team cannot live on praise alone. Its weak points need to be shown up so they can be strengthened. And the same goes for schools. However good we think we are, constructive criticism can help us improve.

Heavenly Father, help us to respond creatively to constructive criticism, not to sulk and take offence but to seek more full and perfect lives. Amen.

The Last Battle

In recent years there's been a glut of magazines and periodicals on sale about wars. In almost any newsagent's shop you can buy pictures of tanks, histories of the development of firearms, aeroplanes and battleships and a summary of the strategy and tactics of most conflicts.

Of course there have always been wars. At first these were quite primitive, the soldiers using swords and shields, bows and arrows. But over the years with progress—if 'progress' here is the right word—of technology more devilish and sophisticated weapons have been employed. One of the nastiest inventions was gunpowder. From that everything seemed to follow, through tanks and shells to grenades and poison gas right up to the terrors of the atomic bomb and the hydrogen bomb. It's a depressing fact that at all times there's a war in progress somewhere on earth.

This seems to point a very gloomy picture of mankind as a race of beings who are dedicated to the destructive and negative tasks of inflicting pain and suffering on themselves. But just as wars have always existed so has man's desire to see the end of all wars. Prophets, teachers and writers have never failed to stand up and preach about a time in the future when all strife will cease and peace will reign on the earth.

One prophecy talks about a last battle called Armageddon—a cataclysm at the end of time when God and his angels will do battle with the Devil and the forces of evil and overthrow them for ever. This is a myth, a parable, a story if you like. And it's meant to indicate the timeless truth that however fierce the struggle may be the final word is spoken not by evil and violence but by love.

Heavenly Father, we pray for those who suffer as a result of war, and we ask your gift of peace for the whole world. Amen.

The Law of Contract and the Grace of God

You can't go very far in today's world without coming across the word 'contract'. Everybody who works has a contract of employment. If your parents wish to sell the house, they'll have to exchange contracts with the buyers. In the mid-1970's there was talk about a so called social contract. In fact the word turns up almost wherever we look. What does it mean?

Well, a contract is an agreement—usually a written agreement. And it's there to ensure that no one takes unfair advantage of another person in employment or business affairs. Even teachers can't just be given the sack at a moment's notice. They have a contract of employment which entitles them to, say, a term's notice. And this means also that a teacher or any other employed person mustn't simply walk out of his job. He is obliged by his agreement to give reasonable warning. To do otherwise would be to break or breach contract. And contracts are agreements binding in law, very serious and important documents signifying arrangements which shouldn't be broken. So if a man enters into a really important agreement with another, he often asks for the agreement to be put in writing—that is for a legal contract to be drawn up.

Now surely there's nothing more important on earth than man's relationship with his creator, with God. But astonishingly when we look at what the New Testament says about God we find that there's no formal, stiff and starchy contract at all. God doesn't say, 'I'll accept you if you're good but I'll throw you out if you're bad,' He says that no matter how unhappy with ourselves we are, however much we think we've failed, he always loves us. And that's something beyond contract. It's called 'grace'.

Heavenly Father, give us generous and forgiving hearts that we may love others as we are loved by you. Amen.

Leviathan and the Fish Hook

Why do innocent people suffer? It's fairly easy to adjust to the idea that if you do wrong you'll be punished or even if you put your hand in the fire you'll burn it. But what about tiny babies who can't even talk? They've had no chance to learn anything. Certainly they've had no opportunity to do wrong and deserve punishment. They're not even old enough to know the difference between right and wrong.

And then there's the innocent civilian casualties in every war. They didn't ask to fight. They didn't ask to be bombed. What about young men and women who die at the very beginning of promising careers—perhaps even leaving orphaned children? Why doesn't God stop these unfair things from happening?

The answer is that there's no answer at all. At least not an answer that everyone agrees on. The Bible contains a book which is a story about a man called Job. Some people reckon that the story of Job's life is one possible solution to the problem of innocent people's suffering.

He's a good man. Yet God allows him to lose all his possessions, his family and friends until near the end of the story poor Job sits by himself covered in boils, sick almost to the point of death. Naturally he wonders why he's been made to suffer such a fate.

And in this parable God answers Job out of the whirlwind: 'Where were you when I laid the foundations of the earth?' and 'Canst thou draw out Leviathan with a fishook?' Leviathan was the mighty sea monster which Job's people feared. And in this story the writer is saying that the purposes of God who made all there is including the earth's foundations and Leviathan are beyond the understanding of men. God allows evil for a good reason which is not revealed to us in this life. We must trust him. To some people this is no answer at all. But perhaps in the end it's the only solution we have. You must make up your own minds.

Almighty God, Help us when we suffer not to forget your love. Amen.

A Lovely War

It's amazing how good people are at giving to charities. And poppy day is one that hardly anyone refuses. Every November we see a poppy wherever we look. It's in a good cause too—the care of old and wounded servicemen. But there are some who say we should do away with the annual festival of remembrance. That we should ban the poppy. They don't say this because they have no concern for those who suffer in world wars. Quite the opposite.

Those who are against the remembrance services say that they only serve to glorify war. That they make us think war is something great and noble. Something fine and good. And you must admit they have a point. All those displays by the armed forces, the uniforms, the drill, the tanks and the guns can encourage in us a feeling that fighting is glorious. Often the patriotic tunes that are played at the same time build up this sense of glory.

But it isn't like that at all. It's about men dying in mud and filth. Children and young mothers being blown to smithereens by bombs and shrapnel. It's about pain and blindness, paralysis and fear. It also shows us how capable we are of hating and doing to one another the vilest of things in the name of politics or country—or God even.

Some years ago there was a musical written called *Oh What a Lovely War*. It was designed to make fun of all those noble attitudes towards fighting. The writer used well known hymns, songs and marches connected with war but he put different words to them—words which revealed the true horror, dirt and torture of every battle. Many of those who respect the pageantry of remembrance services are outraged by *Oh What a Lovely War*. But perhaps neither side ought to be angry with the other. For if we use *every* reminder of war (whether it's a satirical musical or a poppy) to teach ourselves afresh that every battle brings suffering, then we might one day manage to banish fighting forever. We might at least stop to think before we fire.

Almighty God, comfort and heal those hurt in wars. Help us to live in peace. Amen.

Missed by Lightning

We're always being warned about the danger of standing under trees during thunderstorms—you could get struck by lightning. It's not very likely that many of us will be killed in this dramatic way. The chances have been calculated at over two million to one against. All the same, you can't be too careful. There's no use in asking for trouble. If you ever play golf you'll be at a slightly greater risk—just through being out in the open country for so much of the time. In the early 1970's the champion golfer Lee Trevino was struck by lightning while playing in a tournament.

There was once a French writer called Simone Weil. She remarked on the fact that if someone is *missed* by lightning by a few feet, they're likely to say a very sincere prayer of thanks to God. But if you're missed by lightning by half a mile, it's very likely that you'll think no more about it. Well you might argue why should you give the matter a second thought? Half a mile is a long way, after all. But Simone Weil's point is really all about being thankful—not just for obvious things but for all kinds of gifts and wonders we usually take for granted.

It's easy to be grateful for a large present. For a good holiday or even a day trip to the seaside. It's usual for people to pray for their relations and friends who've fallen sick. And then to be thankful when they recover especially if the illness or injury is a dramatic one—like a car crash or something.

But just look at the things we take for granted, that we hardly ever give thanks for. Usually we're fit. Most days we have some breakfast *and* some lunch *and* some tea. Perhaps we don't need to go to the extreme of thanking God every time we survive a thunderstorm—when we've been missed by lightning. But we do have food and friends and fitness. Let's thank God for them.

Heavenly Father, thank you for all the beauty of the world. For our food and friendship. For our health and strength. Amen.

Mr Miller's Prayers

If you try to think of names of religous books you're more than likely to hit on such titles as *Pilgrim's Progress* or *The Book of Common Prayer*. Or even the Bible. But it would be a mistake to imagine that only books with 'holy' titles have anything to teach us about religion.

In fact, religious belief is so widespread that very many authors have something to say about it—even if it's only that they're against it. In all those stories about being down and out in nineteenth century London, Charles Dickens mentions God. Well you might think that's fair enough. Charles Dickens writes about justice for the poor and surely God's got something to do with that.

But religious belief can't be kept in a tidy corner and labelled 'for Christians only' or 'Holy rules for do-gooders'. God is not restricted in this way. In an extraordinary novel written by a man called Henry Miller you can find this passage:

'We grope for ladders, forgetting that we have wings. We pray as if God were deaf and blind.' Henry Miller is trying to tell us to have more faith in God. To trust him because he created us and is always with us even in our blackest moments. The book is called *Nexus*.

So perhaps you'd think that Mr. Miller is a Christian preacher, a Vicar or something like that. But you'd be wrong. In fact he doesn't claim to be a Christian at all or to speak for any particular religion. And yet to have written words like that Henry Miller must have experienced belief and faith and trust very deeply.

This of course goes to show that God isn't just concerned with churchgoers—he certainly isn't limited by them. But that he uses all men and women to reveal different aspects of his nature and purpose. And that trust in him is one thing we should have in plenty.

Almighty God thank you for speaking to us of your presence through many and different people. Help us to trust you, knowing you are always with us. Amen.

The Multicoloured Swap Shop

The biggest market place in the world is to be found in any school playground. Not much money gets exchanged but *goods*—real goods like pictures of aircraft, comics, games and books—are passed round and bartered according to a long standing custom. The custom of swapping. Sometimes the swaps are at an expensive level of which Sothebys might be proud: 'My camera for your skate board.' 'These binoculars for that cricket bat.' But usually the deals aren't in this big league at all.

Older teachers—aren't *all* teachers old?—might tell you about swapping cigarette cards and glass marbles. Maybe such things still go on. And that's a good thing because so often we see old traditions dying out and not being replaced by much that looks worthwhile.

For instance, going to the cinema, or the pictures as it used to be called, seemed to decline during the 1960's. Families stayed at home to watch television instead. So many local cinemas were forced to close down or be turned into warehouses or bingo halls. In fact the television gets its share—perhaps more than its share—of blame for the decline of old traditions. You'll hear people say, 'Ah, in the old days we didn't spend our time staring at a box in the corner. We used to play cards and darts and dominoes.

Well it's probably true that there's a lot of material of doubtful quality on the television. Certainly it's wise to pick your programmes and not just watch whatever happens to be on—or flicking from channel to channel out of boredom and the want of anything better to do.

But marvel of marvels! What do we find on the box on Saturday mornings? Yes, *The Multicoloured Swap Shop* of course. Like the biggest school playground in the world. And just proving that television doesn't always destroy traditions. Sometimes it preserves them. D'you know, you could swap almost anything you liked. I heard of one bloke trying to swap his sister.

Heavenly Father, help us to rule the television and not the television to rule us. Thank you for programmes like *Swap Shop* which preserve our valuable traditions. Amen.

No Escape

The worst kind of dream is the one where you're being chased by some big ugly monster and your legs just won't run. On top of that there's a wall in front of you thirty feet high and on either side there's tall fencing with barbed wire on the top. It's awful. There's no escape—except to wake up, put on the light and wait for your thumping heartbeat to slow down again.

And it's not just in horrid dreams and nightmares where there's no escape. Take the idea of God for instance. Some people believe in God. They say prayers to him and perhaps go to church on Sundays. They think that God acts as a help and a guide in their lives. Their religion adds purpose and meaning to their own existence. But then something awful happens—a serious injury or perhaps some close relative or a friend dies unexpectedly.

What happens then? Well the belief in God and prayer often takes a pretty heavy jolt. Some even stop believing altogether when some tragedy like this comes upon them. But here's the part where there's no escape. For if evil occurrences are a stumbling block which prevents people from believing in God, then good and happy happenings are a problem for the person who does not believe.

There's no getting away from the fact that if you believe you will at some time in your life experience severe doubt. But there's no escape either from the equal and opposite fact that if you decide there is no God you will from time to time come upon hints—perhaps in nature; maybe in a deep friendship—which seem to point to the existence of a good God. There's no escape but there is a prayer about it. Maybe it's a help!

Lord I believe, help thou mine unbelief. Amen.

Pangloss, noses and spectacles

The reason we have noses is so that we have something to balance our spectacles on. That, or something like it is what a teacher called Pangloss says in a novel called *Candide* by Voltaire. Pangloss was fond of saying that this is the 'best of all possible worlds'—that everything has a purpose and, come what may, everything that happens, happens all for the best.

52

Now Voltaire was a satirist. That means he made fun of accepted ideas and established authorities. You know how Jonathan Swift satirised politicians in his *Gulliver's Travels*—saying that their arguments were about as important as disputes about which end of a boiled egg to crack. You don't have to agree entirely with Swift to enjoy his book, but it's easy to see what he's getting at.

It's the same with Voltaire, except that he was ridiculing certain religious teachers and churchpeople who didn't take the fact of evil and suffering in the world seriously. They argued, 'It's all for the best'. Such an argument won't do of course because there's no denying the presence of real and horrible suffering which afflicts millions in the world every day. Voltaire's book is a catalogue of earthquakes, fires, tortures, murders and disasters. His hero and friends suffer one tragedy after another. But these sufferings are just part of a story, and in any case, they're so utterly extreme as to be unbelievable and so we laugh. This doesn't do away with the fact that, lurking behind Voltaire's satire—his comedy of suffering—there is a problem.

If God is good why does he allow his creatures to suffer? What is God's purpose with the world? Those who offer simple answers to these deep questions deserve to be satirised and made fun of. The problem of evil in the world has never been solved by anyone. But if there is a God, then even pain and suffering must have *some* part in his plan. Christians see an illustration of this mystery in Christ on the cross.

Heavenly Father, help us to bear suffering and to look after others when they are in pain. Teach us patience and faith. Amen.

Pennies From Potter

Most people like some pop music. That's why it's called 'pop'—short for popular. It's interesting to see how the pop music of each generation seems to have a quality all of its own. The 1970s will be remembered for 'soul' and 'rock' and for so called 'progressive' pop music as well. The '60s' belonged to the floppy haired Beatles and the flower power music from San Francisco.

In the 1930s the flavour was romance and fantasy. Songs like *Love is the Sweetest Thing* and, perhaps the most popular of all *Pennies from Heaven* were all the rage. At a time of slump and depression when millions were unemployed and poor, it's not surprising that people should turn to songs which offered an escape from the hard and dreary life of everyday. They did this through films—the spectacular Hollywood musicals and above all by listening to popular songs and pretending that the fairy tale world these presented was reality—if only for an hour or two.

In 1978 the B.B.C. produced a series of plays by Dennis Potter. The title for the whole series was *Pennies from Heaven*. Potter contrasts the harsh world of a sheet music salesman and his girl friend, an unemployed teacher, with the romantic world of popular songs from the 1930s. But Dennis Potter isn't just inventing a dream world out of his own wishful thinking. He seems to claim that deep down—under all the suffering of everyday life, under all the worry and boredom—the songs tell the truth. They point to a world where people can be happy and full of joy. But he doesn't ignore suffering and illness and death. He says we can only reach true happiness and lasting joy by accepting the fact of suffering in the world. And he does this through a song as well—one played on the street corner by a sick man with an accordion. It's called *There is a Green Hill Far Away*. And that's about Good Friday.

Heavenly Father help us to bear suffering bravely and never to lose hope. Amen.

The People's King

Buckingham Palace must be a splendid place to live in. Countless rooms marvellously decorated. Servants all over the place. Food and entertainment fit for a Queen or a King. As a matter of fact the English Royal Family don't live in the lap of luxury day in and day out. Compared with the magnificence they could enjoy if they wished they eat fairly simply and use only a small part of the palace.

Not all Kings and Queens live as simply as our monarch. And this was especially true in ancient times. Egyptian Kings enjoyed immense splendour even carrying their life style with them to the grave through the construction of the gigantic pyramids.

At Christmas we worship Jesus as King. What kind of splendour did he enjoy? Instead of a palace and servants galore he had a stable for his home and in place of a royal fanfare to announce his birth he lay in a manger among the animals.

Matthew tells us that very important kings came to visit the Christ-child in the stable. But perhaps the most appealing story in the New Testament is the account of the shepherds' visit.

These men weren't famous. They didn't dress in fine clothes and bring expensive gifts. The shepherds came out of the hills around Bethlehem where they'd been minding their sheep. And in his gospel St. Luke tells us how the great news of the Saviour's birth was given to them by the angels.

This holds a great lesson for us. Our faith, the Christian Religion, isn't just for posh people or for the rich. By the fishermen he chose for his friends Jesus taught us that the good news is for everybody. This truth was first shown at his birth when rich and poor alike came to pay homage to the King.

Heavenly Father, help us not to judge other people by how rich they seem to be or how well they dress. Amen.

Philosophy and Fun

It must be nice to be a great and witty person. To spend your time wandering the country wherever you pleased—eating and drinking, getting into good conversations with all kinds of people, listening to music. There can't be many people who could afford such a life these days. But a couple of thousand years ago anybody who was anybody never regarded his education as complete unless he'd travelled.

If you had a really interesting time on your travels you might want to write it all down in a book when you finally returned home. Well, there was a man called Samuel Johnson who lived in the eighteenth century and who went one better. He did all the enjoyable travelling around the country and managed to get someone else to write an account of it all. The man who charted Johnson's adventures was called Boswell. Now Johnson was almost always in good company. He loved witticisms and clever remarks of all kinds. According to Boswell someone said to Samuel Johnson in April 1778: 'You are a philosopher, Dr. Johnson. I have tried too in my time to be a philosopher; but I don't know how, cheerfulness was always breaking in.'

And you don't have to look far these days to get the idea that thinking about the world and man's place in it—that's philosophy—is a gloomy and uncheerful thing to do. If the way some philosophers write their books is anything to go by then philosophy must be the dullest and most miserable study possible. But Johnson was a philosopher and he wasn't dull. Just read Boswell's book and find out for yourself. Maybe the one thing that's absolutely necessary for all philosophers is that they develop a sense of humour, of fun—because when you can't solve all the 'why?' problems in the universe you need to be able to laugh at yourself even for trying!

Heavenly Father, give us wisdom and understanding. Help us never to lose our sense of fun. Amen.

Planet of the Apes

One of the most popular and entertaining films in recent years was *Planet of the Apes*. If you've seen it you'll remember that in this story the roles of man and ape are reversed. The monkeys are the civilised intelligent ones and the humans are regarded by these creatures as lesser beings. Just the opposite way things really are.

Of course, if you're any good at natural history, you'll know that the careers of men and apes have always been closely connected. In fact, more than a hundred years ago naturalists demonstrated that men and women are descended from the monkey family. No doubt you've heard the joke that it's more obvious in some cases than others!

But all jokes on one side, it's astonishing that there still remain a few religious people who think that this doctrine of evolution is contrary to the work of God. They argue that Genesis, the first book of the Bible, tells us that God made men and women just as they are all at once. So one day there were no people and the next there were Adam and Eve grown up and speaking a language. This belief has provoked a great deal of argument and ridicule between some religious people and folks who are scientifically minded.

In fact, there's no need for fear, ridicule or misunderstanding on either side once we see that the doctrine of evolution and the Adam and Eve stories aren't meant to be opposing scientific theories about man's origin, but they are each telling us something true in different ways.

Evolution tells us how man came to be as he now is—through a long history of development which began with the smallest creatures. Genesis assures us that mankind is under the care of God. Evolution is a piece of natural history. Adam and Eve is a living myth meant to convince us that we're not at the mercy of an impersonal universe which goes on and on like a machine but that the origin of all things, God, is personally involved in our lives.

Heavenly Father, help us to recognise that science and the Bible teach us different truths. Amen.

Pleasure and Pain

Do you think there's more pleasure in life than pain? Or is it the other way round? Perhaps the answer might depend on when you were being asked the question. In the middle of a funfair, an exciting cup-final or a seaside holiday it seems obvious that life is very enjoyable—very pleasurable. But if you've got bad toothache or a stomach upset then all the world appears to be an utterly horrible and painful place.

Is there any way of stepping back and taking a detached look at pains and pleasures in the world—of adding up enjoyable experiences and trying to balance them against unpleasant ones? Like a scientist taking an accurate measurement.

A writer called Schopenhaur once said that there is definitely more pain than pleasure in the world. If we disagree he asks us to compare the feelings of one animal engaged in eating another with the feelings of the animal being eaten.

A vicious and gruesome scene! And whatever we think about Schopenhaur, there's no denying that the world can be a very cruel place. Besides the warlike activities of men and women, states and nations, there's the constant occurrence of floods, pestilences, famines, earthquakes and dozens of other natural catastrophies. We spend much of our lives in avoiding pain, sickness and injury only to know that we must all face death in the end however we live.

And yet people still desire to go on living. Not just for the next pleasure which will relieve our present pain either. Frequently when folks talk about pain and pleasure they're referring to quantities of delight or dismay. The great religions of the world don't talk about quantity at all. They are concerned with quality. We cannot expect constant pleasure and maybe we believe that there's a great deal of pain in life. Our only way of finding satisfaction in the world and some degree of happiness is to see in it a greater significance and meaning than is to be found in passing pleasures.

Heavenly Father, thank you for our enjoyment of life. Please give us your help when things are painful and difficult. And teach us to trust you and your creation through good and evil alike. Amen.

Police Call

In the 1970s police programmes became very popular on the television. Not films about actual police work, but dramatic series about individual policemen. *Starsky and Hutch. Serpico. Ironside. McCloud. Cannon.* All these showed the fast moving American version of law and order. In a different style *Dixon of Dock Green, Z Cars, Softly Softly* and *Task Force* presented the British slant. Then there was *Maigret* the French detective and of course *Charlie's Angels* introducing the lady policeman or the policewoman. One series was actually entitled *Policewoman*.

Now in an age when television drama series explore every possibility it's only to be expected that a programme about the police will turn up. But a score or more of such programmes makes you think that there must be a bit more than simple coincidence at work. Why did all these series develop at roughly the same time? They're exciting and fast moving of course. Many present glamorous stars in the leading roles. But any programmes could do that so why choose the police every time?

If somebody said it was all to do with our belief in angels, everyone would laugh at him. It's not fashionable to believe in angels these days. You'd be ridiculed as 'stupid' or 'soft' if you claimed to believe in those delicate cherubs with wings that turn up on the Christmas cards. And even more stupid if you tried to say the police were anything like that, because of course they're not.

But not all angels look like fat babies with gossamer wings. In many ancient stories they are strong spirits which band together to defeat evil and preserve good—like a police force in fact. Perhaps in an age when people find belief in spiritual beings difficult the police series give body to our need for guardians.

Heavenly Father, give us peace in our towns and cities, in our minds and hearts. Amen.

The Pressure on Pilate

The gospels tell us that Jesus appeared before Pontius Pilate the Roman Governor. Under the law in Palestine, only Pilate, the representative of Caesar, could pass the death sentence on an accused prisoner. So those who argued for Jesus' crucifixion needed the Governor's signature.

When we read the account of Jesus before Pilate, it seems fairly obvious that the Roman official is convinced that Jesus isn't the dangerous rebel that some soldiers and leading Jews were suggesting. So why allow him to die? Why permit the execution?

It's not as simple as that. Many factors were at work in the scheme of events which led to Jesus' death. There was the intense jealousy which the Jewish leaders had in the face of Jesus' popularity with the people. Then there was the suspicion on the part of the military people that Jesus was a dangerous rebel likely to take arms against the occupying power. Finally there was the fact that Jesus himself didn't prevent his followers making statements about his nature and mission. And this led to one misunderstanding after another. All these factors combined to make Jesus' position impossible.

Even then though you might think that once he came for trial before Pilate, the governor would see that there was no harm in him and let him go. Unfortunately, affairs had run too far ahead for that. The leading Jews, envious of Jesus' popularity, played on the fact that the crowds were hailing him as a king. The truth was, of course, that Jesus referred to his kingship in a spiritual sense—the kingdom of Heaven. But to Pontius Pilate the idea that anyone was setting himself up as king meant only one thing—rebellion against Caesar. Even when he could see that this was not so, the Jewish leaders kept insisting that if Pilate let Jesus go free then he was collaborating with enemies of the Empire. Pilate knew that this kind of accusation would result in his recall to Rome, the loss of his job and perhaps even worse. So he bent under the pressure and Jesus went to the cross.

Heavenly Father, when we are called upon to make important decisions, help us to choose what is right and not take the easiest way out. Amen.

The Punctuation Marks of Music

Some of the most dramatic sounds in all music are made by the percussion section of the orchestra. Drums, cymbals and the rest. So these are often used at the beginning or at the climax of a piece. And because of this someone once referred to percussion instruments as 'the punctuation marks of music.' It's easy to imagine a thump on the drums as a full stop. Or the clang of cymbals as an exclamation mark.

We're always being told how important it is to punctuate properly, otherwise our sentences might be misunderstood. And so music probably needs its punctuation marks too. But no one would go so far as to say that commas and stops are the most important part of writing. You couldn't tell a good story in semi-colons and question marks alone. And yet we need them to be there—not too obviously, not where they're not wanted—but there all the same. That's how it was with the orchestra for a couple of hundred years or so. But some modern composers aren't prepared to let percussion play this small part. Musicians like Peter Maxwell Davies and Karlheinz Stockhausen use these instruments to do more than just add the dots and commas to a piece of music. Perhaps they've been influenced by jazz which has always used percussion in a big way.

So, far from being given simple punctuation jobs to do, drums, gongs and cymbals are, if you like the expression, being asked to form nouns and verbs—and sometimes whole sentences in musical compositions. Some people don't like this new trend but many think the newly promoted percussion adds excitement and drama to music. Try listening to *Music Now* or *Music in Our Time* on the radio and notice how Beethoven has been forced to move over—by a drum roll!

Heavenly Father, thank you for all kinds of music. For all the instruments and the different sounds they make. Teach us to listen to them all and to enjoy what we hear. Amen.

Punk

Somebody said that those teenagers in the 1970s who wore safety pins through their cheeks were no better than savages. They said that Punk Rockers were untidy and obscene—filthy even. That they'd no sense of decency or responsibility and the music was awful as well. The very names they chose for themselves and their rock groups showed that they had no taste whatever. How about 'Johnny Rotten and the Sex Pistols' for instance?

Well, of course, it might all be true and these young people really a disgrace to their generation—to all decent and upright people. Proper people with 'standards'. But then they said the same about 'The Beatles' in an earlier age. Press cuttings from the 1960s show that all the insults recently hurled at the Punk Rockers were once used on the group who wrote *Eleanor Rigby* and *She's Leaving Home*.

Ten years before that it was 'Bill Haley and the Comets' who were supposedly corrupting the young. Adults wrote of how shocked they were by this crude and disgusting music and how those teenagers who were fans of Bill Haley were no better than animals. It's a funny thing but these same adults who were once so critical can often be seen these days listening with great enjoyment to the music they used to despise. Perhaps this shows that they're just hypocrites. More likely that they just didn't understand. That pop music is a thing that really belongs to young people and those who are older will always take more time to get used to it. Eventually they'll like it—but it won't be pop by that time!

Is it a possibility that pop music, when it's really new, is a kind of protest on behalf of young people? Protest at having to live according to the rules of a society which they had no part in forming. And that 'Punk' like the earlier 'Rock and Roll' is a picturesque way of saying 'Look, we've got our own lives—our own music too!'

Heavenly Father, help us to work and play honestly. Not to criticise where there is no fault. And not to be angry without a reason. Amen.

Room 101

Imagine being forced to spend a lengthy period in a locked room with what you fear most. For some this might be spiders—large hairy spiders with long grey legs. Or slithery poisonous snakes with beady eyes and evil tongues. A million squeaking mice dancing round your legs. Poison gas. Suffocation. Daggers. Needles. Ghosts. The list is endless. No doubt you can think of your own example.

In his book about a possible and terrifying future called *1984* George Orwell creates such a room and gives to it a number—101. It's a place for enemies of the state. And a main character is put in it as a punishment to be confronted by his greatest fear—rats. Filthy, germy, verminous, infected rats. Needless to say this is the most harrowing part of this exciting but disturbing story.

Being confronted alone with the object of your greatest fear is a fantasy that all makers of horror stories dwell on from time to time. It doesn't matter what your particular terror is—being drowned, buried alive, hanged or guillotined—the fiction writers can portray it.

But terror isn't, unfortunately, limited to fiction. Everyday life has horrors of its own. Guilt. Anxiety. Loneliness. These are just some of them. Ancient people used to think that there were what they called evil 'powers and principalities' which caused the worst kinds of suffering. These were thought to be invisible spiritual beings—utterly wicked in their inmost natures. The New Testament says that Jesus has triumphed over these powers and principalities. Whether or not we choose to people the universe with spirits in modern times, it remains true that the Christian Faith provides a comfort, a defence and a victory over evil.

Heavenly Father, teach us to trust that nothing can separate us from your love. Amen.

Sad and Old?

There must be thousands of people who used to go to church but now don't go any more. Ask them if they still believe in God and most will very likely say they do. So why did they stop going to the church? Surely that's the best place to worship God? In a quiet and reverent atmosphere and in the company of other believers. But they'll tell you—those who stopped attending church—that the people who do go are sour faced and unfriendly. That the vicar preaches boring sermons. The tunes are slow and drab. On top of all that the place smells slightly moth eaten and it's cold.

A lot of church people would want to contradict that view. 'It's not like that at our church' they say. 'Our services are cheerful and we sing bright hymns with modern tunes. Afterwards we go for a coffee in the parish room and everybody gets to know one another.' And they'd be right in some cases. But the fact remains that many people are put off church because it's often dull and gloomy, boring and monotonous.

A Frenchman, Georges Bernanos, wrote in his book *The Diary of a Country Priest:* 'Look: I'll define you a Christian people by the opposite. The opposite of a Christian people is a people grown sad and old.'

But those who've left the church would disagree with him. 'No, Mr. Bernanos' they'd reply, 'You've got it all wrong. It's the Christian people who are sad and old—at least in the churches we've been in.' Why is it then that so many churchfolk look and act as if they're full of misery? Perhaps it's because over the years of habit they've got used to going to church week in and week out. They think about the building, the state of the roof, the plumbing, the garden fête, raising money. And all these things have become a great burden to them, completely squashing the joy which they once expressed in worship. So they have grown sad and old. You can get like that about schools as well as churches. That's not what Jesus intended. He was the one who said, 'I have come so you can have life and a full life at that.'

Heavenly Father, give us a full life. Save us from ever becoming sad and old at heart. Give us love, joy and cheerfulness. Amen.

Saturday Night Fever

All the rage in 1978 was a film called *Saturday Night Fever*. It was about dancing—modern dancing not the old fashioned stuff they used to do in the old ballrooms. The star of the film was a boy, a marvellous dancer the centre of everybody's attention. The world of the dance floor was romantic, glossy and exciting. Here the dancer was a real star—a hero.

But the film might well have been renamed 'Saturday Night Fever—Monday Morning Blues.' For the world of the everyday outside the dance hall was very different. When the music stopped the fun ended as well. Many of the young people who lived glamorous lives on Saturday night were unemployed on Monday morning. They lived in a large city, in an unfashionable area where housing was bad and jobs hard to get. It might have been a good idea to film the dance hall in colour and the rest in black and white to illustrate the contrast between the Saturday excitement and fever and the weekday gloom.

Some people disapprove of young people staying out late dancing. They reckon that there's too much violence and danger attached to dance halls and discos. Certainly there's plenty of violence in the film *Saturday Night Fever*. Some scenes aren't fit for adults, never mind children! But it should be seen and everyone should take notice of it. For a film like this shows what great skills young people can develop and what a power enthusiasm is. The dancing is superb.

The sad part is that all this expertise and enthusiasm is wasted on the ordinary weekdays. And the message is that energy unused will not just dry up—evaporate. If human beings aren't given the chance to be useful and constructive, they will use this energy in destructive and violent ways—not just on Saturday night but all through the week.

Heavenly Father, we pray for the unemployed, especially for teenagers who have no work. And we ask you to guide all those who make decisions which affect jobs and careers. Amen.

The Scream

Not all films are nice to watch, but then most of us enjoy scaring ourselves silly so why worry? People will sit through the most terrifying and dreadful scenes. Bodies rising from graves. Men swinging from gallows. A lady being stabbed while taking a shower. It's not even as if we don't know what we're in for. The titles of the films ought to warn us clearly enough. *Dracula Has Risen From The Grave*, *The Murderer's Fate* and *Psycho* to name three too many for some people.

Surprisingly, there are even a few teenage children who can't sit through this sort of film. Girls of fourteen who turn cold at the sight of blood even when they know it's only tomato sauce. Big boys from the football team who prefer to look at the stake going through the vampire's heart—but who would rather squint at the horrible sight through fingers placed protectively before the eyes.

64

Some even scream. If you go to a cinema where they're showing one of these sorts of films you'll hear many a scream. Some in fun, because we all like to pretend, but others screech at the shock experienced as the headless ghost appears. Can you remember how you felt when you last screamed? Startled? Terrified? Unable to move and literally scared stiff?

In a famous picture by Edvard Munch—it's called *The Scream*—there's a woman on a bridge yelling in absolute terror. There were those who said that it didn't look like a picture of a real woman at all—or even a real bridge. But many more people are fascinated by Munch's picture because it reproduces what we all feel like inside when we scream. And that's what the painter intended. Not to reproduce faithfully a likeness of a screaming woman but to put on canvas where we can see it the very inner feeling which goes with screaming. He expressed outwardly what was inside himself at a particular moment. Artists like Munch are called Expressionists. One thing at least they show us is that inner experiences are just as real—if not more so—than the solid objects which go to make up the outside world. Perhaps even more real than a vampire's coffin lid.

Heavenly Father, make us sensitive and aware of other people's feelings and help us to cope with our own. Amen.

Singing in the dark

People are sometimes tempted to stay off school even when there's not much wrong with them. Obviously we shouldn't come when we've got flu and spread our germs to everyone else. But some would stay away for a pain in the little toe. You can divide folks into two lots—those who can put up with pain and discomfort and those who can't. It's easy to tell which is which. The bad patients will soon let you know who they are. Let them get a cold and they slouch around dragging their feet and moaning about their head pounding, the stuffed up nose, the poor sore chest and the frozen back.

Those who can stand a bit of suffering and not let it get them down aren't as easy to spot—largely because they don't make a song and dance about their illnesses. Notice they look a bit off colour and try to sympathise? They'll soon tell you 'It's nothing, just a touch of the sniffles. Be gone in a couple of days.' And they don't let it interfere with their work and play.

The difference between those who can tolerate suffering and those who can't is seen in a more extreme form when we think of people who are severely handicapped. Some take to their beds or never go out of the same room. They feel defeated by their affliction—unable to cope with everyday life. Perhaps they think that life or fate or God has been unfair to them. 'Why should I suffer like this? What have I done to deserve this?'—questions often asked. And you have to sympathise because it does seem unjust that, while most of us have all our arms and legs and normal movement, some are crippled, others may be deaf or blind.

One thing is certain: however badly handicapped a person may be, he has a much better chance of triumphing over his disability if he determines it isn't going to spoil his life or make him bitter. Of course it's easier said than done. But we do have examples to help us—men and women who suffered terrible tortures and starvation in times of famine and war. Young people who triumphed over spastic disability and won good degrees at the university. My favourite is George Handel the composer who went blind but still carried on with his music. In fact he wrote a song about blindness. Handel really showed us how to deal with suffering—by singing in the dark.

Heavenly Father, teach us to bear our sufferings cheerfully and not to be beaten by pain but to look for some way of turning it to good. Amen.

Sit Still!

There can't be a pupil in any school anywhere who hasn't been told at one time or another to sit still. And true enough it's a great annoyance to a teacher trying to get some difficult point across to his class when he finds that two or three bodies in front of him are wriggling about. It looks untidy and worse still it makes a distracting sound.

In a poem called *Ash Wednesday* T. S. Eliot wrote 'Teach us to sit still.' Well, you might think it's fairly important to keep quiet in class sometimes but surely it's going a bit far to ask God to teach me the knack? And quite right. But Eliot meant something quite different. What he really intended is clear when we see what comes before the line: 'Teach us to sit still.' The poet writes:

'Teach us to care and not to care.'

Clear? It doesn't look all that clear. To care and not to care. That's a contradiction isn't it?

But there's another way of looking at the poet's statement. Perhaps he really meant 'Teach us to care about the things we can affect by caring. Teach us not to care about those things we can't possibly do anything about.' When we read it like that the poem seems clear enough.

And if you've ever seen parents, teachers or friends rushing about, anxious and worried about a thousand things at once—or if you've been weighed down yourself by difficult problems, you'll know what T. S. Eliot's poem means. Because we all fuss and fluster and worry about those things we can't change. And unfortunately, we sometimes don't do as much as we might about the problems we can deal with. Perhaps when we sort out the difference between them we shall be able to follow that next line and sit still.

Almighty God, please help us to care and not to care. Teach us to sit still. Amen.

Sounds from Life

In 1791 Wolfgang Mozart died. He is one of the most famous composers of all time. His works—almost a thousand of them—include pieces for choirs, orchestras, chamber groups, all the solo instruments with church music and opera besides. It would be impossible to try and say which piece out of all these compositions is the best. But one is rather different—the piano concerto in G major K.453. The 'K' stands for 'Köchel' the surname of the man who arranged Mozart's works in rational order after the composer had died.

One tune in this concerto was inspired by a pet cage bird which Mozart kept at one time. Perhaps he was specially fond of the bird and wished to commemorate it in a permanent way and that's why Mozart wrote the creature into his concerto. Maybe the composer simply liked the bird's tuneful whistle and so borrowed its tune for his music. No one knows for certain.

Other composers have used natural sounds in their music. Beethoven pictured a storm in his *Pastoral Symphony'*. More recently Edward Cowie has taken birdsong of the part of north Lancashire where he lives and used that in his compositions.

This isn't to say that you'd immediately recognise Mozart's bird from K.453. Or that the *Pastoral Symphony* reproduces the sound of a real storm. And Cowie's music isn't a tape recording of local birdsong. It is to say that the sounds heard and referred to by these three composers have had some effect on their musical creations. If you like, the sounds of nature have been inspirations.

Here's something which seems to be true of all works of artistic creation in music, words or pictures. The artist takes his raw material from the world as it is and changes this into something new through his talent as musician, writer or painter. Simple reproduction could be achieved through a machine like a tape recorder. It needs an individual act of reshaping on the part of the creative artist before we can hear or see his contribution to our understanding of the world.

Heavenly Father, help us through words, paintings and sounds to appreciate more fully the richness and complexity of the world you have made. Amen.

A Spectacular Revelation

There have been thousands of good films made. And perhaps even hundreds of really excellent ones. Just which ones you're prepared to place in the first rank depends quite a lot on personal taste and preference. Devotees of the 'horse opera' will no doubt choose films like *Gunfight at the O.K. Corral*, *The Magnificent Seven* or the classic *High Noon*. Then there's *Reach for the Sky*—Douglas Bader's story for all the World War II fans. *Love Story* got terrific audiences didn't it? And *Star Wars* really packed them in.

There's a lot to be said for making films out of Bible stories. It's been done about Moses in *The Ten Commandments*—the bit where the Red Sea parts is the best. And hundreds of films on the life of Jesus have been made in glorious technicolour. But I don't know if anyone has ever filmed the story you can find in the last book of the New Testament. It's called *The Revelation of St. John*. And what's in it? It'd be more appropriate to ask what's *not* in it! There are beasts with seven heads, angels holding vials of wrath, dragons, plagues, earthquakes and finally a golden city in a perfect square coming down from heaven to make a new paradise.

It's all picture language of course. Poetry if you like. One man's views of what the end of the world might be like. But what a terrific picture it would make.

Now in the middle of all the bottomless pits and lakes of fire you can find in the *Book of Revelation*, there's one utterly mysterious sentence. It says: 'There was silence in heaven for about half an hour.' What a thought! What were they waiting for? It doesn't say. You'll have to imagine . . .

Heavenly Father, thank you for imaginative writers. Help us to see in the word pictures they use something of your glory. Amen.

Spies and Invisible Ink

If books and films about James Bond are anything to go by, then being a spy is a marvellously interesting job. Dangerous maybe but never boring. Spies travel to exotic locations often to meet even more exotic characters, eat the best food, drive the most glamorous cars, fly aeroplanes and kill off their evil opponents with incredibly spectacular gadgets.

Who wouldn't be a spy then—even after allowing for the danger? In fact this James Bond version of spying is a big fantasy. Really espionage agents live a most unglamorous existence—working in offices and factories. True enough it's still a dangerous profession. But the danger involved is of a quiet, unsensational kind. Imagine being a spy at I.C.I. or the Inland Revenue Department of the Civil Service! A bit of a come down from the Far East or the missile sites of Cuba.

And yet there's still hope for those who like to think that spying is more of an exciting game than a rather tedious chore. In 1977 the French newspapers announced that they'd arrested some spies. Where? In a nuclear power station? No. In a secret rocket base? Of course not. But in a Government Department. 'Well' you might say 'there's nothing very exciting about that.' But wait for it—the authorities found among all the briefcases and documents which they took from the foreign agents—invisible ink. Now that's more like it. Spies and invisible ink! Real spies caught using every young boy's favourite party trick. And to think we were all ready to say goodbye forever to romantic ideas about spying. But foreign agents using invisible ink—makes you almost believe the days of James Bond's magic gadgets are on the way back.

Heavenly Father, thank you for unusual and fantastic events. Please help us to cope with the ordinariness of life as well. Amen.

Stripey White Lines Don't Hurt As Much as Buses

In the middle of York, just before you get to the railway station, there's a very dangerous bend. You can tell it's dangerous because the Highways Section of the Department of the Environment have painted some stripey white lines in the middle of the road. These are meant to be a warning: 'Keep left. Don't drive over these lines because the road narrows and bends and becomes dangerous.'

Now you'd think every driver would be grateful for such a warning. It could save your life. And probably most drivers are glad of the guidance these white lines offer. But it's not as simple as that. Nine times out of ten as you come round that bend there's a bus parked on the left—sticking out a mile from the kerb. So all the drivers are forced to pull over to the middle of the road and therefore across the lines. It's understandable really because stripey white lines don't hurt as much as buses.

Now this might seem a trivial example. Or if not trivial at least one that could be settled by whoever is responsible for road markings in the city of York. But it's more than that. It's a sort of fable or parable about human behaviour or morality.

Here's the issue in a nutshell. When you're told a rule such as 'Keep off the stripey white lines' should you *always* obey that rule even if it leads to bad consequences like running into the back of a bus or holding up the traffic all over the town? Not a big issue perhaps since it's only about a road sign. But what if the rule is 'Do not kill'? Obviously most killing is wrong and avoidable. Most killing is called murder and that's defined as *wrongful killing*. But what about a war where an evil and aggressive dictator threatens to wipe out millions? Would it be right or wrong to kill him? And were the Jews right to kill the terrorists in Uganda? Most people would agree they were right. The point being that rules can't decide everything for us. Sometimes we have to make decisions in the light of events.

Heavenly Father, we ask your blessing on Parliament and on all those who make rules for our good. Give them wisdom and right judgment. Amen.

A Stroke of Luck

Once there was a farmer who took his gun out with him on the tractor. He did this every day and never gave the matter a second thought. One day though the tractor hit a bumpy patch and the gun was let off by accident. The poor farmer was shot in the leg. Eventually someone came to his aid and he was taken off to hospital. There he lay for a long time and unfortunately his leg had to be amputated in the end. But he was a courageous man and never gave up without a struggle. So he practised hour after hour until he could walk on the artificial leg which the surgeons provided for him. He walked well on it too. You'd never think he even had an artificial leg—just a slight limp.

In time he was able to return to his work on the farm. Years passed and the farmer approached middle age. One day he had a mild seizure or 'stroke' as it's sometimes called. This illness often has the effect of temporarily paralysing one side of the body. The farmer had to take things easy for a few months—doctor's orders. But after a while he was able to get up and about again—though he wasn't ready to start work on the farm for many months.

One Sunday morning after the church service the farmer approached the vicar in the vestry. And here, referring to his stroke, he made a highly original and amusing remark. You remember that strokes tend to paralyse? Well the farmer said, rejoicing, 'If I hadn't had a wooden leg I wouldn't have been able to walk.' The vicar took careful note for a sermon about good coming out of evil.

Things don't always work out as well as that. There's a lot of evil in the world which doesn't seem to have its good side at all. Take earthquakes and floods for instance. But it remains true that with courage and perseverance and above all with a sense of humour, even the most testing difficulties can be overcome.

Almighty God we ask for your blessing upon the sick and all who tend them. We pray for courage and faith when we are ill that we may never give in to pain and suffering. Amen.

Superman

Sometimes, if you're lucky, there's a *Superman* programme on the television on a Saturday morning. If you're unlucky then you may have to put up with *Batman* or the *Bionic Woman*. They're not bad but not anything like as good as Superman. They can at least in theory be destroyed but Superman is absolutely invincible—unless the mad villain can find himself a piece of kryptonite.

It's interesting to note that the Superman idea didn't start off in Hollywood or in the mind of a television producer. In a book written a hundred years ago the philosopher Frederich Nietzsche described the superman. The book is called *Also Sprach Zarathustra*. Nietzsche wasn't writing about our superman of film and television fame of course but about the kind of man he thought was the most admirable. The sort of person we ought to try and become.

According to Nietzsche the superman is above common men. Not just in having more strength and energy but he doesn't share ordinary man's weaknesses at all. He rejects the ideas of sympathy and pity. One day he sees a beggar weeping and bemoaning his state. Zarathustra (the superman) takes a whip to him and administers a severe beating as a punishment for what he regards as grovelling weakness. Of course the superman doesn't believe in God. He accepts nothing or no one as being greater than himself.

It's significant that the only real superman—a person so wonderful and amazing that he's attracted the worship of hundreds of millions over twenty centuries—was the very opposite of Nietzsche's creation. I'm talking about Jesus Christ. He told us to love our enemies as well as our friends, to have mercy and pity on all men, and to regard self-giving as the highest—the most super-activity available to man.

And it's a strange fact but Jesus has been regarded as the greatest of men—as God on earth by Christians—just because he lived out and preached the way of life open to all men: loving, forgiving and self-giving. Perhaps, after all, Superman is best kept in his S-suit on Saturday T.V.

Heavenly Father, thank you for the life of Jesus Christ. Help us to be generous and self giving. And give us grace to forgive when others offend us. Amen..

Terror and Zeal

In recent years the world has seen more than enough terrorism. The trouble with this kind of protest is that innocent people become involved in military and political power struggles whether they like it or not. It's not your choice if your holiday plane is hijacked. And it's not the fault of young children if they're caught in crossfire between the army and guerillas.

In case we imagine terrorism to be a fairly recent development it does no harm to remember that the old pattern of guerilla warfare was well established by the time of Jesus—even that, indirectly, it helped to bring about his crucifixion.

This may seem strange to us. After all we've been brought up on the stories of Jesus as a kind and gentle person who went about doing good. What possible link could there be between terrorism and 'gentle Jesus meek and mild.'? Well it's certainly true that Jesus spent much of his time teaching and healing—that he was a man of peace. But it didn't always appear like that to the authorities.

And that's because at the time of Jesus, his country, Palestine, was under Roman rule. The Romans were very stern and strict and if they noticed large crowds collecting they were immediately suspicious. Thinking that crowds might be guerillas or private armies of Jews bent on the overthrow of their rule the Romans would arrest the ring leaders and crucify them. This was to frighten the followers into disbanding. The ring leaders were known as zealots.

It's well known that Jesus frequently collected a large crowd around him. These were usually people who wanted to hear his teaching and have Jesus heal their sick friends and relations. But the Romans couldn't afford to take chances especially as they knew that the political revolutionaries called zealots would likely infiltrate the crowd.

So the answer seemed simple. Get rid of Jesus and a lot of trouble would be avoided. And as we know this is what they did. It's not the whole story of course but suspicions of Zealot activity was one of the causes of the crucifixion of Jesus.

Heavenly Father, help us to avoid misunderstanding the motives and actions of others. Amen.

Thales and the wine presses

The greek philosopher Thales was walking through the woods. Not looking where he was going at all. But, as philosophers do, he was gazing up at the stars. His mind on heavenly things. Suddenly he fell into a well. Everyone laughed as they pulled him out. 'That's philosophy for you', they said 'no use whatever. Let that be a lesson to you!' But Thales got his revenge.

He heard that the olive crop was likely to be extra good one year. So he bought all the wine presses in the area. When the harvest came and everybody wanted to crush the olives for oil they had to go to Thales and pay the price that *he* asked for the presses. Nice way of getting your own back. Made a lot of money as well. Proved that philosophers can apply themselves to everyday concerns when they need to.

The word 'philosophy' comes from two Greek words which mean 'love' and 'wisdom'. So a philosopher is someone who loves wisdom in the sense that he regards it as life's richest treasure. And he will sacrifice everything in his search for it. Money, power, fame or friends may be important, but to the true lovers of wisdom they are not the main things in life.

Maybe this sounds bookish and stuffy. Imagine spending all your life in a world of ideas. Thinking. Reasoning. Working out logic and arguments. Wouldn't it be better to go to the pictures or spend a day at the seaside? It must be an odd sort of chap who sets out to be a philosopher. It seems a bit like being a monk.

But there are other ways of seeking wisdom—and even perhaps finding it at last. That's the way not of turning your back on ordinary life but of living it thoughtfully. We've all been called 'dreamers' and 'scatterbrains' from time to time—that's when we've not been concentrating on what we're supposed to be doing. There's room for daydreaming. And there's wisdom in the life of everyday. Thales and the well. Thales and the wine presses. Heavenly thoughts; practical wisdom.

Heavenly Father, thank you for the marvels of your universe. For the sun, the moon and the stars. Teach us wisdom in ordinary earthly things. Amen.

Thanatos The Unthinkable

'Thanatos'—it's just a Greek word for death. Comes in very useful for horror film producers. In one late night movie there was a ghastly place filled with bodies and tortures. They called it 'Thanatos Palace.' Posh language for 'House of Death.' This was deliberately done of course, but it's amazing what lengths people will go to in order to avoid talking about death. Real death not death on the screen.

Evelyn Waugh wrote a very funny book called *The Loved One*. He mocked the American funeral trade which makes a fat living out of trying to deny death. So dead bodies are called 'Loved Ones' and those who are still alive are known as 'Waiting Ones'—as if we've nothing more important to do than hang around waiting for death. What an insult! Not by Evelyn Waugh though but of those funeral directors who protect us from all mention of death and dying presumably because they think we're not mature enough to think about these things.

In *The Loved One* coffins are called 'caskets' and places where the bodies are stored before burial are 'Slumber Rooms'. Lots of special people work in this cemetry called 'Whispering Glades'—people called 'hostesses' and 'cosmeticians'. The whole aim is to prevent us from thinking of death as something which happens to us all and which is so often a cause of unhappiness and distress.

Of course it's no use pretending that real death and real dying don't exist. And it's downright dishonest and distasteful to refer to corpses and funerals as if they're anything other than what we know them to be. At the same time we shouldn't become preoccupied with death so that we talk about it and think about it all the day long.

The great religions of the world teach us to face up to the fact that one day we're all going to die. But they don't tell us to be gloomy and morbid about it. Instead we should live our lives to the full in the service of what is good and true and holy. And then we shall not fear death but recognise it as a natural event. No one knows what comes after death but Christians believe that nothing can separate us from the love of God—not even death itself.

Heavenly Father, teach us to give ourselves to your service, to all that is good and true and holy. Be with us when we are afraid. Amen.

Titilating Titles

Treasure Island is one of the most exciting books ever written. And it's been made into films and television serials more times than you can count. You can't forget characters like Long John Silver and Blind Pew or rhymes such as:

'Fifteen men on a dead man's chest
Yo ho ho and a bottle of rum.'

But what is it that makes you want to take this book from the shelves and actually start to read it? It's a long way from page one to the back cover. The title has a lot to do with it. *Treasure Island* really grabs your interest. But nobody could get enthusiastic over an alternative title such as *The Possibility of Financial Gain in Remote Areas Surrounded by Water*.

No it's the title that gets us to pick up the story and start to read it. What's the most exciting title you can think of? *Twenty Thousand Leagues Under the Sea*? *The Creatures from the Black Lagoon*? *Dracula*? Perhaps something else altogether. One thing's certain: H. G. Wells would never have sold many copies of *The First Men in the Moon* if he'd called it *Primary Manifestations of Anthropoid Existence on a Proximate Natural Satellite*. Perhaps even *Dracula* wouldn't have done too well under the title *New Techniques in Blood Transfusion*.

Book titles are just a few samples of language being used in an interesting and appealing way. There are the advertisements for foreign holidays: 'Sun' 'Fun' 'Sand and Sea' appear all over the place next to words like 'glorious' 'exotic' and 'Panoramic.' In the same way, football commentators use instant sentences like 'The Brazilian striker blasted the ball into the back of the net.'

What a pity then when so much bright language is there for us to use, boring words get written and spoken instead. Like 'interfacing' instead of 'matching up'. 'At this moment in time' in place of 'now'. And most boring of all 'situation'. There's never any need to use the word 'situation'—unless of course you're advising people never to use it.

Heavenly Father, thank you for the gift of language. Help us to use words clearly and imaginatively. Amen.

Traitor!

In the story of Jesse James the outlaw we see that the sheriff and his men can never catch him. So they hire one of Jesse's friends Robert Ford to do their job for them. And Robert Ford, coward that he was, shot the wanted outlaw in the back.

There's something about a traitor that puts us off. Even, as in the case of Jesse James, when the wanted man is a dangerous outlaw we don't like the idea of betrayal. It's sneaky and cowardly. It offends our sense of fair play—the kind of honest to goodness conflict two gunfighters have as they walk towards each other on the main street at high noon.

How much worse then when the person who's betrayed hasn't even done anything wrong. This is so in the case of Jesus when his whereabouts were revealed to the Romans by Judas Iscariot. We want to ask, 'Why did he do it? What had Jesus done to cause Judas to betray him?'

It might have been for money—the Bible says that the Romans paid him thirty pieces of silver. But this doesn't seem all that likely. After all, Judas could have taken the money which Jesus and his disciples carried around with them. The Bible also tells us that Judas was in charge of the purse.

It seems much more likely that Judas betrayed Jesus because of frustration and disappointment. In the years that he'd been part of the close band of men and women who'd followed Jesus, he'd seen the popularity of both man and message. Everywhere Jesus went large crowds gathered to hear him speak. They began to hail him as the Messiah—the chosen one of God who was to deliver the Jewish people from oppression.

Perhaps Judas was one of many who saw this deliverance in political terms—as if Jesus would gather an army from the crowds and overthrow the occupying Roman power. And when it became absolutely clear that Jesus had no intention of taking that course, maybe out of desperation Judas turned him in to the authorities. A more likely explanation than that the keeper of the purse should betray his friend for thirty pieces of silver.

Almighty God, give us the courage and the strength always to be faithful to our friends even when they let us down. Amen.

A Truth Universally Acknowledged

Five minutes in any school playground is enough to convince you that it often seems as if agreement is the hardest thing in the world to reach. Everybody has his own opinions. About everything or so it seems. It's not just religion and politics where argument never ends, but pop music, fashion, football, television programmes and a thousand other issues.

So it seems odd to read a statement of universal or worldwide agreement. But that's the way *Pride and Prejudice* the name of a story by Jane Austen begins. Here's what she writes:

> 'It is a truth universally acknowledged that a single man
> in possession of a good fortune must be in want of a wife.'

Of course, Jane Austen is being gently sarcastic—having a dig at those leisured ladies in their eighteenth century finery who spent all their time looking for a husband. She really meant us to understand that all young ladies in the best circles wanted to marry into riches. If any truth was 'universally acknowledged' then that was it. Authors of novels are allowed to use extravagant language and to make claims that can't really be justified in fact, so long as what they write increases our enjoyment. *Pride and Prejudice* is, after all, a work of fiction designed to entertain and amuse us.

But back in the real life of school and work we know that no one's opinion is accepted as 'a truth universally acknowledged.' Argument, discussion and debate are everywhere. And this is a good thing too. For without the stimulation of disagreement and opposition there could be no genuine progress in human knowledge. Every new thought is always a reaction to someone else's old thought. And wisdom is the result of reasoned argument and an ability to see more than one side to every issue. Perhaps that's the only truth that does deserve to be 'universally acknowledged.'

> Heavenly Father, teach us always to examine problems with the knowledge that there is more than one side to every question. And help us to learn from those who hold views which are different from our own. Amen.

Two Deadly Sins in the Football League

If you watch the B.B.C.'s *Match of the Day* you'll soon notice that commentators remark about two particular faults of the players. One is a footballer's reaction to another player who trips him or commits a late tackle. It's a temper tantrum. Anger. Perhaps as a result of provocation. But anger nonetheless. We're all used to seeing this kind of thing. United's striker runs into City's penalty area and, just when he seems to have a clear sight of goal, he's brought down from behind by a vicious tackle. In many cases he responds fiercely—sometimes even with fisti-cuffs. A clear case of anger.

The other criticism by football commentators on T.V. is that often a player doesn't have a good work-rate. He doesn't run and tackle as much as he should. He's lazy. Or as it says in the book of Proverbs, his attitude is best described by the word 'sloth'.

Of course anger and sloth aren't just confined to the football field. Anyone can be lazy. Anyone can lose his temper. In fact in Christian Doctrine these two faults are regarded as being so common that they're listed as two of the 'Seven Deadly Sins'. It's worth noting just what exactly is sinful about them. For it's not always wrong to be angry. When for instance, someone behaves irresponsibly and causes a lot of hurt to other people, then maybe the judge, the teacher or the parent has a right to be angry. In the same way, it's not always wrong to hang about doing nothing in particular.

No, the sinful side of 'sloth' and 'anger' comes when they're displayed at the wrong time. For example, if I take things easy when others are depending on my hard work. Or if someone lashes out angrily in the face of a criticism or telling-off which he thoroughly deserves.

Heavenly Father, teach us always to do the right thing at the right time and to know when to keep silence. Amen.

Visiting Cards of God

The early Jewish people lived in the deserts of the Middle East. There the sun burned down all day. Water was scarce. And night brought icy temperatures and a clear black sky. Night and day were cold and hot stillnesses following one another without relief. Almost without relief, but not quite. For occasionally the loose sand on the surface of the desert would begin to curl slowly and eerily as if by magic. This was only the prelude to that most fearsome desert phenomenon—the sandstorm.

This was the very trademark of terror. Whirlings and burning exposed limbs, eclipsing the torrid midday and turning the whole desert into a swirling hell from which there was no relief. Luckily such storms didn't last very long.

How odd then that the Jews should imagine that the storm was a dwelling place of God—even that the wind was his breath. And yet that's just what they did believe—that God was not always a gentle caring shepherd. Sometimes he was a fierce driving wind. True enough the wind served to help the Jews from time to time. As at the Exodus from Egypt when the Bible records that God drove back the Red Sea by a strong east wind. But such a mighty force was certainly beyond the power, strength and influence of the desert people.

The Jewish belief shows that men and women don't usually go in for creating kind, friendly and manageable gods who never raise any dust. Instead human beings have always taken the untamed and hostile aspects of nature and said, 'Yes, God is in these as well.' Almost as if the wind is a sign of God's presence—like a visiting card.

Heavenly Father, protect all those who venture into extreme weather in order to go about their daily work. We pray particularly for all sailors and fishermen. Amen.

The Wasp With the Wig

Adventure books are great favourites among young readers. There's *Treasure Island*, *War of the Worlds* and *The Three Musketeers* to name only three. But most people of whatever age also like an impossible story. Tales by Edward Lear. And perhaps the most famous of all fantastic and crazy stories *Alice Through the Looking Glass*, by Lewis Carroll.

What strange and incredible characters there are in that book. The White Knight who keeps falling off his horse and shouting 'Check.' Humpty Dumpty with his tie—or is it a cravat? And of course the Red Queen herself. When *Alice* first came out over a hundred years ago one of the most striking attractions of the book was the illustrative work. An artist co-operated with Lewis Carroll and drew a picture of each and every one of the characters who feature in the story.

Now here's something you perhaps didn't know because it's only recently been discovered. There's a missing chapter to *Alice Through the Looking Glass*. Well, it's not missing now because it's turned up! But for many years nobody knew the chapter existed. It's called *The Wasp With A Wig*. And the reason it wasn't included in the book is a rather strange one. The artist who drew the pictures for Lewis Carroll wrote to the author and said he couldn't possibly provide a suitable picture for the chapter so why not leave it out? Lewis Carroll took his advice.

In a much wider sense it's odd how we can give names to objects and yet not be able to picture them. A good example of this is the round square and that's impossible! But it's true also of words like 'God' and 'Heaven' and in these cases we might not think the words stand for impossible objects at all. Perhaps we have a vague picture—an outline only. Maybe that's what Lewis Carroll's illustrator had of the wasp with the wig. But the story exists right enough.

Almighty God, we know that some truths are beyond our under-standing and that the universe is filled with secrets. Thank you for artists and scientists who are gradually showing us more of your creation. Amen.

The Ways of Aquinas

In the thirteenth century there was a famous thinker called Thomas Aquinas. He was a very religious person and devoted his powerful mind to thoughts about God. Not just random, haphazard thoughts but logical, ordered sequences of deductions—like a theological detective.

Aquinas is remembered for his demonstrations of God's existence. Some people even refer to these arguments as 'proofs' as if God could be shown to exist in the same way as you might prove a theorem in geometry.

Perhaps a better word for Aquinas' arguments though is 'ways'. For he never claimed that he could prove God's existence as if he were a mathematical object. But he did say that certain ways of thinking about God could lead a reasonable man to believe in him.

And this is more like the approach we can imagine the Christian God using. He doesn't force anyone to believe in him, but leaves hints and suggestions as to his presence and reality. Some preachers occasionally give the idea that we must believe in God as if he was the last result of a laboratory experiment. Or worse, that if we don't accept God's existence, then something evil will happen to us—eternal punishment in a blazing hell for example.

But this isn't God's way at all. He doesn't compel belief and he doesn't strike atheists dead in their tracks. He gives us a choice. He gives us clues about his being. And he never seeks to overrule our careful thoughts and wonderings about him.

In this God is served well by Thomas Aquinas, for he too has worked out his opinions into 'ways' or 'approaches' to God. These don't have the finality of watertight proofs or commandments to believe. And when you think about this you may realise that it is after all the best way to faith. For simply to demand belief through literal proofs would be to override that most precious of God's gifts to us—independent, enquiring minds.

Almighty God, help us to use our minds to draw closer to you through looking carefully at the world you have made. Amen.

The weight of glory

There was a man who kept fishes. Not just goldfish or sticklebacks and things like that but beautifully coloured exotic tropical fish. He started off with one tank and a small heater with a thermostat fitted so that the water would keep a constant temperature. There were just two simple green plants in the tank and overhead was a plain electric light bulb and a tin shade.

Years went by and the man saved his money and gradually bought more and more tropical fish even more beautiful than the first ones. They had names like 'Swordtail', 'Neon Tetra' and 'Angel Fish.' All the time he studied them and made more and more aquariums for them. He read books about fishes and joined a local society of men and women who had the same hobby. He liked the Angel Fish best because of its long fins and its ability to remain almost motionless in the water.

Now his fish tanks were filled with the most delightful plants and coloured lights illuminated them so that the whole room seemed as if it was enchanted. All the neighbours knew about his hobby and they would often pay him a visit just to look at his beautiful aquariums.

Once a neighbour asked: 'Why do you keep fish? What good are they?' The man replied, 'Why I keep them because they're glorious!'

When religious teachers talk about men and women they sometimes say something very similar. For all our faults, our selfishness and our seemingly endless inability to get on with one another, human beings are glorious as well. 'Glory' means *worth* or *weight*! The Jewish religion and the Christian faith both teach that we are made for the glory of God. Perhaps we don't glorify or give weight to God very much when we argue and fight. But when we use our minds to reason and our imagination to create works of art then we reflect the glory of our heavenly Father. Above all we glorify God when we put aside selfishness and try our hardest to forgive those who hurt us and to love one another.

Heavenly Father, thank you for making us and giving to us bodies, minds and spirits. Help us to love one another, to forgive our enemies and so glorify you. Amen.

The Well Tempered Clavier

Parents and teachers often tell us that nothing that's worthwhile ever comes without effort. If we want to gain the mastery of a school subject or a sport then we have to work hard. This is particularly true when it comes to learning a musical instrument like the piano. If you've ever tried you'll know that even the simplest pieces require much practice. There's scales, arpeggios, fingering, time signatures and more besides. Particularly there's all the separate keys to master.

Now it may sound unlikely—especially when you've just spent an hour in difficult practice—but there was a time when no-one knew about key signatures. Or at least when nobody bothered about them very much.

It was in the early part of the eighteenth century when Johann Sebastian Bach first drew everyone's attention to the system of keys on keyboard instruments. In a large series of compositions called *The Well-Tempered Clavier* Bach wrote a prelude and a fugue in each of the keys: twenty-four major and another twenty-four minor.

A key in music is a kind of starting and finishing point. A place where a tune can end satisfactorily and something in which a melody has a familiar movement from one note to the next. When Bach wrote *The Well-Tempered Clavier* he virtually laid down the rules about how composers should write their music for two hundred years. And you might imagine that laying down the law in this way would be a rather strict, stern and unimaginative thing to do. But Bach's *Forty Eight* as these pieces are called are absolute marvels of tunefulness and musical beauty. Which just goes to show that order and rules in artistic creation don't always mean repetition and boredom. At least they didn't in the case of Johann Sebastian Bach.

Almighty Father, help us to order our thoughts in a good sequence so that step by step we may achieve knowledge. Amen.

Well——Why?

Long ago just about where you're standing now there was a ruin. Part of it was made in crumbling brick but its ancient middle section was pure stone and went back to the time of druids and magic circles. It was said that in the centre of the ruin, between the two tall pillars, was a box containing a scroll on which was written a recipe for everlasting life.

Everyone tried to get at the box. They came from all over the country—from all over Europe even. Rich men, princes. Lords and kings with their slaves and their women trekked to this shrine which was called 'Magdis'. Their one aim was to achieve immortal life. To find the box. Read the scroll. Mix the potion that would guarantee eternal bliss for the finder.

But no one got any nearer than the outer part of the shrine. Past the high gate which connected to an unclimbable wall. Yes some got closer than that only to find that suddenly they were trapped by a strange and eerie force. A force which paralysed their bodies and terrified their minds until eventually they wasted away completely and no trace of them was ever found. A thousand years ago people thought this was the work of an evil demon—though some thought it was the job of a guardian angel to stop men and women returning to paradise.

In the last hundred years or so there have been other theories. For instance that the mysterious and destructive force was really some kind of peculiar electro-magnetic field. Or even that it has something to do with anti-matter.

Now there's nothing wrong with this story—except that not a word of it is true. It's just been made up. But you might ask why do stories like this catch our interest? Well——Why?

Heavenly Father, Thank you for tales of mystery and imagination. Amen.

What Kind of Oracle?

Some people treat the Bible as if it were a kind of magic oracle—a book that provides instant answers for every question. And sometimes these same people will say, with great force, 'The Bible says so and so, etc, etc...' By this kind of statement they'll expect the rest of us to know immediately what course of action to take in even the most difficult moral dilemmas.

D'you know the story about the man who looked at the Bible in this extreme way? Apparently, seeking guidance to get himself out of a spot, he opened the book at random. And the verse he came upon was about Judas. It said: 'He went out and hanged himself.' Clearly this didn't seem to be very constructive advice so he opened it up a second time. There before him it said 'Go and do thou likewise.'

84

It's only a story of course but it tells us one thing for sure. It tells us what the Bible isn't. It isn't a book we can treat as if it was a magical source of all wisdom. We can't take verses out of the context in which they were written and use them for a purpose they weren't intended for in the first place. The fact is the Bible is a kind of library of sixty-six books—all written at different times and by many authors. It would be just as wrongheaded to compare the Book of Leviticus in the Old Testament with St. John's Gospel in the New as it would be to expect a modern poem or novel to resemble in every detail something written by the ancient Greeks.

But properly interpreted, that means trying to gain some insight into what the original writers meant by what they wrote, the Bible has much to teach us. It is a record of the religious experiences of men and women. If you wanted to learn say, how to cook, you wouldn't throw out all the old cookery books and simply start boiling up ingredients without knowing what you were up to. Well, the Bible can tell us a lot about how people from the past have dealt with the problems of life and death, suffering and evil, creation and destruction. Don't throw the Bible out. But don't shut down your intelligence before you begin to read it.

Heavenly Father, thank you for the wisdom of the Bible and other holy books. Help us never to be too proud to learn from them. Amen.

What's the Use of Dying?

Christians call the day of Jesus' death 'Good Friday'. Extremely puzzling. To call the day when a popular religious hero died 'Black Friday' or 'The Evil Day'—that would be understandable. But 'Good Friday'. What's good about it?

When we look at the evidence from the New Testament stories there's nothing encouraging there—or so it seems. Jesus of Nazareth, a popular religious teacher is dragged before the authorities on trumped up charges and put to a cruel death. His friends and disciples are scattered about the country fearful lest the same fate should catch up with them. Jesus leaves his mother broken hearted and his enemies triumphant. What's so good about that? In terms of the world today, Jesus would be called a failure.

We place so much emphasis on getting on, getting to the top. Making ourselves indispensable and well-known. Well-liked and famous. Living in the best area of town. Having all the work saving gadgets in our tidy houses. Taking a good holiday every year. Driving an expensive car. Wearing fashionable clothes. These are marks of success in today's world. According to these visible signs of doing well in society Jesus would score very badly. And yet for the last two thousand years men and women have worshipped him not just as an admirable man but as the Son of God.

The only answer possible is that Jesus, the carpenter's son from Nazareth, showed us the truth about our lives in a way that makes sense—a way we can't escape from. The life and death of Jesus reveals to us that the only way to satisfaction, happiness and fulfilment—or 'salvation' as the New Testament calls it—is through suffering. We can hide from reality, if we're very clever, for a long time behind friends and possessions. We can pretend to ourselves that getting more and more things, seeking one pleasure after another, is the way to personal happiness. Jesus shows us that the proper explanation of the world and of ourselves will involve us in pain and discomfort. We cannot pretend that suffering doesn't exist. Only through facing the dark side of life can we make sense of life. That's what Jesus did one Friday. That's why we call the day 'Good'.

Heavenly Father, help us when we suffer pain. Strengthen us when we are anxious. Amen.

The Womanliness of God

The poet Ted Hughes wrote a book called *Gaudete* (rejoice). It came out in 1977. It's about an unusual vicar called the Reverend Lumb. For reasons perhaps known best of all to Ted Hughes, The Reverend Lumb spends much of his ministry among women. This makes him unpopular with most of the men. Though one man defends him in the pub:

'Old Smayle defends the vicar.
He admires him. The vicar, he declares,
Has realised that his religious career
Depends on women.
Because Christianity depends on women.'

Christianity depends on women? If you look around local churches, you'll probably come to that opinion yourself. It's usually the women who arrange the flowers, keep the church building clean, make themselves responsible for the brasses, the linen, the embroidery. They organise themselves into groups which are often the butt of comedians' jokes but which really do a lot of good around the parish. Groups like the Mothers' Union or the Young Wives. And perhaps most striking of all, two thirds of most congregations are women.

Women have always played a large part in the history of Christianity. The gospels tell us of Mary and Martha. There's the tradition about Veronica who mopped the sweat from Jesus' brow with her handkerchief. That was while he carried the heavy cross to the place of crucifixion.

And yet—for all the space given to women in churches past and present—you can't help coming away with the idea that they're God's second class citizens. After all, Jesus chose men to be his disciples. No New Testament book is by a woman. And many churches today will only ordain men to the priesthood.

Perhaps here the church has got itself out of balance. At the time of Jesus, women played a very secondary rôle in society. But it's not so now. And maybe that means it's high time for the church to reconsider its traditional attitude towards women—they can do all the work *but* let them keep quiet in church.

In Christian teaching God himself in the person of Jesus was born of a woman. And Roman Catholics pray to Our Lady. Isn't it reasonable to suppose that whatever we mean by 'God' has as much 'woman' in his nature as 'man'?

Jesus, born of a woman, help us to rid ourselves of prejudice and to treat all people as human beings made in God's image. Amen.

Name Index

Theme Index

Subject Index